Praise for From STEM to STEAM

"From STEM to STEAM *is a game changer for educators who are serious about bringing excellence back into the classroom. It crosses ages, stages, and curriculum development through research and practical application.*"

—Darleen Horton, Environmental
Magnet School Coordinator,
Cane Run Elementary, Louisville, KY

"*This book is a must-read for educators, policymakers, and industry leaders addressing how to develop an innovative workforce for the future. Sousa and Pilecki have successfully outlined a pragmatic approach to empower teachers with the ability to integrate the arts into science, technology, engineering, and math (STEM) discipline areas. This sets the stage for a national conversation to move from STEM to STEAM.*"

—Edward L. Abeyta, Director of K–16
Programs, University of California,
San Diego Extension, La Jolla, CA

"*Imagine classrooms of children imitating the 'ways of knowing' experienced by DaVinci or Michelangelo. In* From STEM to STEAM, *authors Sousa and Pilecki not only persuade us to integrate arts into the K–12 curriculum, they also remind us of the value of a classical education—an education that reveals how all knowledge is interrelated. In this timely book, the authors entice K–12 educators to transform their classrooms into centers of arts and science inquiry; and, in a rather credible manner, provide step-by-step guidelines for engaging K–12 learners in a rich interdisciplinary curriculum of science, technology, engineering, arts, and mathematics.*"

—Susan Lee Pasquarelli,
Professor of Literacy Education,
Roger Williams University, Bristol, RI

From **STEM**
to **STEAM**

From  STEM
to STEAM

USING BRAIN-COMPATIBLE
STRATEGIES TO INTEGRATE THE ARTS

DAVID A.
SOUSA

TOM
PILECKI

CORWIN
A SAGE Company

CORWIN
A SAGE Company

FOR INFORMATION:

Corwin
A SAGE Company
2455 Teller Road
Thousand Oaks, California 91320
(800) 233-9936
www.corwin.com

SAGE Publications Ltd.
1 Oliver's Yard
55 City Road
London EC1Y 1SP
United Kingdom

SAGE Publications India Pvt. Ltd.
B 1/I 1 Mohan Cooperative Industrial Area
Mathura Road, New Delhi 110 044
India

SAGE Publications Asia-Pacific Pte. Ltd.
3 Church Street
#10-04 Samsung Hub
Singapore 049483

Source of bottle xylophone photo on page 182: Natursports/Shutterstock.com

Printed in the United States of America.

Library of Congress Cataloging-in-Publication Data

Sousa, David A., author.

From STEM to STEAM : using brain-compatible strategies to integrate the arts / David A. Sousa, Thomas Pilecki.

pages cm
Includes bibliographical references and index.

ISBN 978-1-4522-5833-1 (pbk.)

1. Arts—Study and teaching. 2. Science—Study and teaching. 3. Interdisciplinary approach in education. 4. Cognitive learning. I. Pilecki, Thomas, author. II. Title.

LB1591.S68 2013
372.5—dc23   2012046842

This book is printed on acid-free paper.

Acquisitions Editor: Jessica Allan
Associate Editor: Kimberly Greenberg
Editorial Assistant: Heidi Arndt
Production Editor: Cassandra Margaret Seibel
Copy Editor: Megan Markanich
Typesetter: C&M Digitals (P) Ltd.
Proofreader: Lori Newhouse
Cover Designer: Michael Dubowe
Permissions Editor: Karen Ehrmann

SFI Certified Sourcing
www.sfiprogram.org
SFI-00453

14 15 16 17 10 9 8 7 6 5 4

Contents

Acknowledgments

Darleen Horton
Environmental Magnet School Coordinator
Jefferson County Public Schools, Cane Run Elementary
Louisville, Kentucky

Debra K. Las
Science Teacher
Rochester Public Schools
Rochester, Minnesota

Susan Leeds
Teacher
Howard Middle School
Orlando, Florida

Renee Peoples
Teacher and Math Coach
Swain West Elementary
West Bryson City, North Carolina

Herbert Perez-Vidal
Freelance Writer
Retired Professor of French and Spanish
Palm Beach State College
Palm Beach, Florida

Gavin Quinn
Biology and Environmental Science Teacher
Eastern Camden Regional High School
Voorhees, New Jersey

Tracy Rosof-Petersen
Teaching Artist
Lake Worth, Florida

Melanie Sitzer Hedges
Art Teacher, National Board Certified Teacher (NBCT)
West Gate Elementary School
West Palm Beach, Florida

About the Authors

David A. Sousa, EdD, is an international consultant in educational neuroscience and author of more than a dozen books that translate brain research into strategies for improving learning. He has presented to more than 200,000 educators across the United States, Canada, Europe, Australia, New Zealand, and Asia. He has taught high school chemistry and served in administrative positions, including superintendent of schools. He was an adjunct professor of education at Seton Hall University and a visiting lecturer at Rutgers University. Dr. Sousa has edited science books and published dozens of articles in leading journals. His books have been published in French, Spanish, Russian, Chinese, Arabic, Korean, and several other languages. He is past president of the National Staff Development Council (now Learning Forward) and has received honorary degrees and awards for his commitment to research, professional development, and science education. He has appeared on NBC's *Today Show* and National Public Radio to discuss his work with schools using brain research.

Tom Pilecki, MA, is the former executive director of the Center for Creative Education (CCE) in West Palm Beach, Florida, where, for twelve years, he provided professional development to over one hundred teaching artists, preparing them to teach collaboratively with elementary and middle school teachers in all curriculum content areas. With an MA in educational administration, Tom is a former elementary school teacher as well as a choral and instrumental music teacher. His forty-plus years in education include being founder and principal of St. Augustine School of the Arts in the South Bronx, New York, the subject of the Sundance Film Festival Award-winning documentary *Something Within Me* as well as feature segments on *60 Minutes, World News Tonight,* and *The McNeil-Lehrer Report.* His expertise in curriculum writing, implementation, and arts integration brought him to Chicago as curriculum director for six West Side schools before going to Florida. He continues to consult with schools and communities on a national basis.

Introduction

The most beautiful experience we can have is the mysterious—the fundamental emotion which stands at the cradle of true art and true science.

—Albert Einstein,
The World As I See It

Response to Intervention, Common Core State Standards (CCSS), high-stakes testing, differentiated instruction, professional learning communities, and the remnants of the No Child Left Behind Act (NCLB) are just some of the buzzwords flying around the teaching profession these days. The din is very loud and teachers are wondering where to turn next. Now comes STEM. In 2006, the U.S. National Academies expressed their concern about the declining state of education in the United States in the areas of science, technology, engineering, and mathematics (STEM). Among the actions it recommended were improving K–12 science and mathematics education, providing additional training for teachers in these areas, and increasing the number of students entering college for STEM-related degrees. In response to these concerns, Congress passed the America COMPETES Act in 2007, which authorized funding for STEM initiatives from kindergarten through graduate school. Numerous school districts across the country have obtained federal and state funding to support their proposals to increase the quality of STEM education.

Despite good intentions and considerable funds spent to encourage the STEM initiative, progress has been slow. Test results from the 2011 National

Assessment of Educational Progress (NAEP) showed only a slight increase in eighth grade science scores over 2009 (NAEP, 2012). When the NAEP tests asked fourth, eighth, and twelfth graders to use higher-level problem-solving and critical-thinking skills in both real and simulated laboratory settings, they performed poorly. In addition, less than one-third of eighth graders performed at what the NAEP considers to be "proficient" levels of achievement.

In response, national science organizations are developing the Next Generation Science Standards (NGSS) to better prepare K–12 students in the sciences for careers and college. The draft NGSS should go to the states for review, approval, and adoption sometime in mid-2013. Regardless how good the NGSS are, they will do little to improve student learning unless curriculum becomes more meaningful, and unless science and mathematics instruction concentrate more on creative and real-world problem solving—in other words, what working scientists and mathematicians *really* do. The question is how do we do this? What type of activities would increase student engagement, raise motivation, focus on relevant issues, and, most importantly, develop creativity? Oh, wait a minute, that's what the arts do. Integrating arts-related skills and activities into STEM courses could be one very effective way to enhance student interest and achievement. Those schools that have tried it report surprisingly positive results that we will discuss in later chapters.

LOOKING TO THE ARTS

Before we turn to the arts and teachers of the arts for help with STEM, we need to come to grips with a few stark realities. Because there are only so many hours in the school day, one consequence of increasing instruction in the STEM areas has been to decrease instructional time in stand-alone arts classes. For example, music and art classes that used to meet three times a week now meet only once a week. Furthermore, when budgets get tight, the arts are often regarded as "frill" subjects and are thus reduced or eliminated, especially in low-income schools. High-stakes testing in reading and mathematics has further bolstered this regrettable trend. Yet, with some deep reflection, it becomes clear that the thorough study and application of the scientific, technical, and mathematical principles embodied in the STEM subjects require skills that can be significantly enhanced by training in arts-related areas.

After all, the main objective of both art and science is discovery. Scientists and artists work

> **The main objective of both art and science is discovery.**

creatively toward a product. Now, neuroscience adds its discoveries to the mix. Implications from recent brain research findings—like the exciting evidence that creativity can be taught—further support the integration of arts-related topics into STEM courses as well as STEM topics into arts-centered courses. The focus is on encouraging collaboration between STEM educators and those in the arts so that STEM adds the A for arts to become STEAM.

HOW THIS BOOK CAN HELP TO IMPLEMENT STEAM

This book aims to demonstrate how integrating the arts into the STEM areas gives teachers new outlooks and the capacity to provide students the skills they need to be more successful in learning and applying STEM content. It does so first by presenting convincing evidence from research studies in cognitive and social neuroscience that demonstrate how activities associated with the arts enhance creativity, problem solving, memory systems, motor coordination, and analytical skills—all critical elements to achieving the STEM objectives. Second, the book contains classroom-tested strategies and techniques for integrating the arts in STEM instruction. Third, we offer some suggestions for building a professional development program to help STEM teachers work with their colleagues in the arts to create STEAM lessons. In addition, the book will list valuable resources available to teachers in the STEM subjects, in the arts, in arts integration, and for STEAM.

To our knowledge, there is no other book on the market that addresses this topic in depth or explains how brain research supports connecting the arts to STEM subjects. We should make clear that this book is written by two authors who have a combined total of more than eighty years of experience as teachers and administrators in both public and private schools and universities. We are keenly aware of the limitations that many K–12 teachers currently face, such as preparing for high-stakes testing and being restrained by inflexible middle school and high school schedules. As a result, we took these limitations into account when we selected and tailored our suggestions and strategies. The good news is that all these strategies have been used with success in other schools by teachers with similar limitations.

This book will help answer questions such as these:

- How can I develop STEAM lessons if I am not artistic?
- What is a teaching artist, and how do I find one?
- What type of professional development will help me implement STEAM effectively?
- How do I fit collaboration with an arts teacher into my already tight schedule?
- What scientific evidence is there that the arts can help students be better at the STEM subjects?
- Will progressing from STEM to STEAM affect student test scores, and, if so, how?
- Is STEAM compatible with the CCSS?

CHAPTER CONTENTS

Chapter 1. Why STEM Should Become STEAM

This chapter explains how engaging in the arts affects us. It examines how the arts develop cognitive and social growth, enhance creativity, capture attention through novelty, reduce stress, and make teaching more enjoyable. It also explains how arts-related skills support and complement the skills needed to be successful in the STEM areas.

Chapter 2. What Science Says About the Arts and Creativity

In this chapter, we explore what researchers in neuroscience and cognitive psychology are discovering about the brain and learning and how that relates to the arts, STEM, and creativity. It discusses theories about how we think, examines how mind-set has such a powerful influence over student achievement and teacher success, and delves into the nature of creativity.

Chapter 3. Frequently Asked Questions About Integrating the Arts and STEM

STEM teachers who are thinking about giving STEAM a try often have concerns about how this will impact on their work, how it will affect student achievement, and how to get started. This chapter addresses those important concerns and gives some tips on how to start on the road to STEAM while maintaining your other duties—and sanity.

Chapter 4. Implementing Arts Integration in the Primary Grades (K–4)

This chapter looks at how teachers can organize their planning to include arts-related activities in the primary grades. Of course, creativity is running rampant in these early grades, and many teachers are already mixing arts with arithmetic and science. Here are some suggestions that you will find both interesting and productive for primary-level students.

Chapter 5. Implementing Arts Integration in the Intermediate Grades (5–8)

Middle school can be quite a challenge for students as they move from self-contained classrooms to a departmentalized structure. Arts-integrated lessons may make that transition into the STEM subject-centered classes easier because these types of lessons can be motivating and stress-reducing. In this chapter, we offer suggestions for integrating arts-related activities into STEM courses.

Chapter 6. Implementing Arts Integration in the High School Grades (9–12)

No doubt the greatest challenges to integrating the arts into STEM lessons occur in high schools. With tighter schedules than middle schools, getting STEM and arts-area teachers to collaborate is no easy task. But it can be done. How? This chapter offers suggestions gathered from current STEAM participants about how to find the time to create and implement successful STEAM lessons in high school.

Chapter 7. STEAM Lesson Plan Appetizers in Science, Technology, and Engineering

Now we explore actual lesson plans that show the integration of arts into STEM subjects. We call these plans "appetizers" because they are meant to whet your creativity to develop your own STEAM lessons. For convenience, we have separated the sample lessons into two chapters. In this chapter, we present some examples of STEAM lessons in science, technology, and engineering (STE) concepts.

Chapter 8. STEAM Lesson Plan Appetizers in Mathematics

Mathematics teachers know that many students have difficulty achieving in mathematics even though they have the capability to succeed. Integrating the arts into mathematics lessons helps students recognize the practical and real-world applications of mathematical concepts. In this chapter, we present some sample STEAM "appetizers" lessons for mathematics in the hope that teachers may encourage their students to work harder and find new meaning in mathematics.

Chapter 9. Putting It All Together

One point we make is that many STEM concepts, such as energy and force, are covered across multiple grade levels. This chapter shows some sample lesson plans that use a common STEM concept across all the K–12 grades and convert them to STEAM lessons. It also explores what kind of professional development program should be considered to help STEM and arts teachers successfully implement STEAM.

At the end of each chapter you will find a page called Major Points to Ponder. This is an organizing tool to help you remember important ideas, strategies, and resources to consider at a later time.

WHO SHOULD USE THIS BOOK?

This book will be primarily useful to classroom teachers in the STEM areas and in the arts because it presents a research-based rationale for why we should pursue integrating the arts into the STEM subjects to form STEAM lessons. It explains the nature of creativity and shows teachers ways to improve creativity in themselves and in their students. Increasing the options that teachers have during the dynamic process of STEAM instruction also increases the likelihood that successful learning will occur.

The book should also help professional developers who continually need to update their own knowledge base and include research and research-based strategies and support systems as part of their repertoire. Chapter 9 offers some suggestions to help professional developers implement and maintain the knowledge and strategies that STEM teachers will need.

Principals and head teachers should find here a substantial source of topics for discussion at faculty meetings, which should include, after all, instructional as well as informational items. For example, how are we encouraging creative projects in non-STEM classes? In doing so, teachers view the principal as supporting professional growth as an ongoing school responsibility and not an occasional event. More important, being familiar with STEAM and arts integration enhances the principal's credibility as the school's instructional leader and promotes the notion that the school is a learning organization for *all* its occupants.

College and university instructors, especially in the STEM areas, should also find merit in the research and applications presented here, as both suggestions to improve their own teaching and information to be discussed with prospective teachers.

WHAT'S COMING?

Engaging in the arts has numerous positive effects on human brain growth and learning. Exactly what those effects are becomes clear in Chapter 1. It explores how the arts develop cognitive and social growth and boost creativity. We will recognize ways in which arts-related skills support, complement, and enhance those skills that students need to be successful in discovering what the basic understandings of the STEM areas are all about.

Chapter 1

Why STEM Should Become STEAM

It is by intuition that we discover and by logic we prove.

—Jules Henri Poincaré, French mathematician (1854–1912)

We have never discovered a culture on this planet, past or present, that doesn't have art in some form. Yet there have been a number of cultures—even some existing today—that do not have reading and writing. Why is that? One likely explanation is that the cognitive, physical, and emotional activities represented by the arts—dance, music, drama, and visual arts—are basic to the human experience and necessary for survival. If they weren't, why would they have been part of every civilization from the Cro-Magnon cave dwellers of 35,000 years ago to the urban citizens of the twenty-first century? (Please see Table 1.1.)

Table 1.1   Public often sees STEM and the arts as having opposite characteristics.

STEM	Arts
Objective	Subjective
Logical	Intuitive
Analytical	Sensual
Reproducible	Unique
Useful	Frivolous

Science, the scientific method, and mathematics, on the other hand, are more recent developments. Around 4,000 years ago, the Babylonians recorded the motions of the moon, planets, and stars on clay tablets. The ancient Egyptians and Chinese made significant advances in astronomy and mathematics. Variations of the scientific method—as we currently describe it—evolved during the Middle Ages in several cultures. Arts and sciences do not compete; they are complementary. The arts create a very subjective view of the world, while science creates an objective view of the world. A person's brain needs both views in order to make suitable decisions.

Few people will argue against studying the natural sciences and mathematics in the elementary and middle schools, and support remains strong for these subjects—including Advanced Placement courses—in high schools. We wish to make clear that we support initiatives that enhance K–12 STEM courses. Recent data show that although there are 3.6 unemployed workers for every job in the United States, there is only one unemployed STEM worker for two *unfilled* STEM jobs (Change the Equation, 2012). There are many STEM-area jobs going unfilled because we do not have the skilled workers for them. Clearly, we need to improve our teaching in the STEM areas.

However, our concern is that when budgets get tight, some people view music and other arts courses as a drain on the funds needed to preserve STEM—especially science and mathematics courses. They often see STEM and the arts as polar opposites. The STEM areas are thought of as objective, logical, analytical, reproducible, and useful. The arts, on the other hand, are supposed to be subjective, intuitive, sensual, unique, and frivolous. In the budgetary competition between the arts and STEM in U.S. schools, the arts have frequently lost.

Figure 1.1 summarizes a recent report by the U.S. Department of Education noting that fewer public elementary schools are offering visual arts, dance, and drama classes during the decade of 2000 to 2010, a decline many attribute to budget cuts and an increased focus on reading and mathematics (Parsad & Spiegelman, 2012). During the decade, the percentage of elementary schools with a visual arts class declined from 87 percent to 83 percent. Although the decline in the *percentage* of schools offering music is not that great, the *amount of time* devoted to music instruction dropped dramatically, typically from three to five periods a week to just one or two.

The drop in drama was larger, from 20 percent to only 4 percent in the 2009–2010 school year. Dance slid from 20 percent to just 3 percent in that same time period. Although dance and drama/theater dropped dramatically during the decade as stand-alone subjects in elementary schools, they

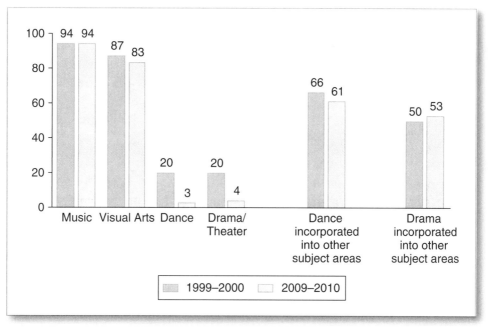

Figure 1.1   Percentage of public elementary schools with arts classes 1999–2000 and 2009–2010.

continued to be incorporated into other subject and curriculum areas. Music classes at the elementary and secondary schools remained steady, but there were noticeable declines in the nation's poorest schools. Just a decade ago, 100 percent of the poorest high schools had music classes, while today that number is down to 81 percent.

THE POWER OF THE ARTS

Many scientists, mathematicians, and engineers know that the arts are vital to their success, and they use skills borrowed from the arts as scientific tools. These include the ability to do the following:

- Draw on curiosity.
- Observe accurately.
- Perceive an object in a different form.
- Construct meaning and express one's observations accurately.
- Work effectively with others.
- Think spatially (How does an object appear when I rotate it in my head?).
- Perceive kinesthetically (How does it move?).

These skills are often not expressly taught as part of STEM courses, but they are at home in writing, drama, dance, painting, and music.

The Real Purpose of Schooling

We should remember that the real purpose of schooling is to prepare students for their life *after* high school, whatever their choice may be. Too often, we look at schools as mainly college preparatory institutions. But we should keep the following statistics in mind:

> **The real purpose of schooling is to prepare students for their life after high school.**

- Almost 25 percent of students enrolled in U.S. high schools drop out *before* graduating (Chapman, Laird, Ifill, & KewelRamani, 2011). What will they do? Will what they learned in high school help them succeed?
- U.S. Department of Education surveys show that in 2009, only about 70 percent of high school graduates went on to college (U.S. Department of Education, 2011). That means that about 30 percent go into the workforce or some other field of endeavor. Are they adequately prepared?
- A growing number of students drop out of college in their first or second year. What will they do next?

We will discuss more about high school instruction in Chapter 6. Our point now is that, although we encourage all students to get as much formal education as possible, providing all high school students with exposure to arts-related activities may give those who do not go on to college the incentive to pursue opportunities in the arts or arts-related fields. Numerous well-known artists in all fields never went to college but became famous for their artistic work nonetheless. A few examples are Ansel Adams (photographer), Ben Affleck (actor), Edward Albee (playwright), Irving Berlin (songwriter), James Cameron (director), Tom Cruise (actor), Bil Keane (cartoonist), and Claude Monet (painter).

The Arts Are Basic to the Human Experience

As we learn more about the brain, we continue to find clues as to why the human activities required for the arts are so fundamental to brain function (see Figure 1.2).

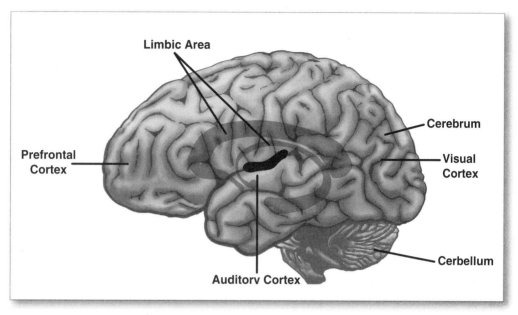

Figure 1.2   Diagram with parts of the brain mentioned in this section labeled.

- *Music:* It seems that certain structures in the auditory cortex respond only to musical tones.
- *Dance:* A portion of the cerebrum and most of the cerebellum are devoted to initiating and coordinating all kinds of learned movement, from intense running to the delicate sway of the arms.
- *Drama:* Specialized areas of the cerebrum focus on spoken language acquisition and call on the limbic system (the emotional control center) to provide the emotional component.
- *Visual Arts:* The internal visual processing system can recall reality or create fantasy with the same ease.

Meanwhile, the prefrontal cortex of the frontal lobe—the brain's executive control area—coordinates all this information to help the individual make appropriate decisions.

These cerebral talents did not develop by accident. They are the result of interactions over thousands of years between humans and their environment, and the continued existence of these talents must indicate they contribute in some substantial way to our survival. In those cultures that do not have reading and writing, the arts are the media through which that culture's history, language, mores, and values are transmitted to the younger generations and perpetuated. They also transmit more basic information necessary for the culture's survival, such as how and what to hunt for food and how to defend the village from predators.

Consequently, the arts are an important force behind group survival. For example, due to its fractured landscape, about 1,000 of the roughly 6,500 languages on this planet are spoken in just one place—New Guinea!

> **Our brain has developed elaborate neural networks to process both language and music as forms of communication.**

Each language is totally unrelated to any other known language in New Guinea (or elsewhere) and is spoken by a tribe of just a few thousand people living within a 10-mile radius. Even more astonishing is that, despite their isolation, each tribe has its own music, visual arts, and dance (Diamond, 1992). These arts-related activities give the tribe its identity and its individuals a sense of belonging.

In modern cultures, the arts are thought of rarely as survival skills, but rather as frills—the aesthetic product of a wealthy society with lots of time to spare. In fact, people pay high-ticket prices to see the arts performed professionally, leading to the belief that the arts are highly valued. This cultural support is often seen in high schools, which have their choruses, their bands, their drama classes, and an occasional dance troupe. Yet seldom do public elementary and middle schools enjoy this continuous support, precisely when the young brain is most adept at refining the skills needed to develop artistic talent (several private school initiatives have been the exception, most notably the Montessori schools and the Waldorf schools). Furthermore, when school budgets become tight, elementary and middle level art and music programs are among the first to be reduced or eliminated. Now, pressure to improve reading and mathematics achievement is prompting elementary schools to trade instruction in the arts for more classroom time in preparation for high-stakes testing. Apparently, state testing programs believe it is much more important for a student to know the letters that make up words and sentences but not the notes of the scale that produce a melody. Yet our brain has developed elaborate neural networks to process both language and music as forms of communication. Why would that be if both were not biologically important (Sylwester, 2007)?

This trade-off does not make sense in light of the emerging research on how the arts assist in developing the young brain. We will first explore the arguments for teaching the arts—whether they be taught as separate courses or infused with other subjects, or both—and then suggest how including the arts can help students be more successful in learning the concepts associated with the STEM subjects.

Why Teach the Arts?

The basic arguments we make here are these:

- The arts play an important role in human develop-ment, enhancing the growth of cogni-tive, emotional, and psychomotor pathways in the brain.

> ***The arts develop . . . creativity, problem solving, critical thinking, communications, self-direction, initiative, and collaboration.***

- Schools have an obligation to expose children to the arts at the earliest possible time and to consider the arts as a fundamental—not an optional—curriculum area.
- Learning the arts provides a higher quality of human experience throughout a person's lifetime.
- The arts evoke emotions, and we know that emotions enhance learning and increase retention.

The skills that the arts develop include creativity, problem solving, criti-cal thinking, communications, self-direction, initiative, and collaboration. All these skills—which align with what many educators now refer to as "twenty-first century skills"—will be needed by every student in order to survive successfully as an adult in an increasingly complex and technologi-cally driven world.

The Olympics Once Honored the Arts

Walter Winans' first Olympic medal in the 1912 Summer Olympics in Stockholm was the silver medal for sharpshooting (Stromberg, 2012). When he took the winner's podium a second time, it was to receive a gold medal awarded for a small bronze statue of a horse pulling a chariot. Winans had won the first ever Olympic gold medal for sculpture. How did this happen? Baron Pierre de Coubertin, the founder of the modern Olympic Games in 1894, was well aware that the ancient Olympic Games in Greece included contests of art, and they were equal in prestige to the sports competitions. By 1912, he was able to convince the Olympic committee to include medal awards for works submitted in the areas of music, painting, architecture, literature, and sculpture. The only condition was that the work had to be inspired by the concept of sport.

The awards continued for nearly four decades, but were discontinued after the 1948 games. Ironically, the Baron's idea still lingers. For the 2012 Summer Olympics in London, artists were invited to send sculptures and graphic works on the theme "Sport and the Olympic values of excellence, friendship, and respect." No medals were awarded, but the winners received cash prizes, and their work was displayed in London during the games.

Even today, the arts are important to the Olympic Games. Just think of how the arts are needed in designing the winners' medals, the venues, the logo, the torches, the cauldron, and the athletes' outfits; in designing and making the costumes and directing the choreography for the opening and closing ceremonies; and in writing and selecting the music for the ceremonies and gymnastic competitions. The Olympic Games still place value on the arts; shouldn't our schools do the same? Figure 1.3 shows the major reasons why we should ensure that the arts remain available for all students at all grade levels.

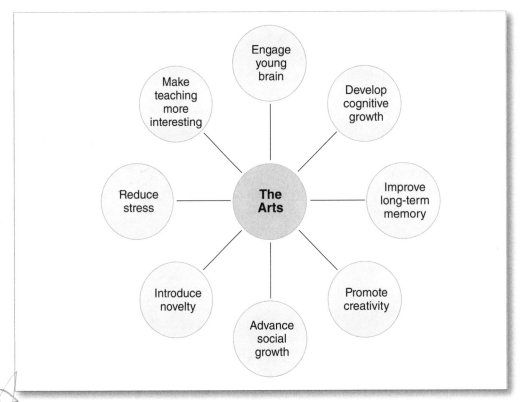

Figure 1.3   The diagram illustrates the reasons why the arts should remain available for all students at all grade levels.

The Arts Engage the Young Brain

During a child's early years, there is an explosive growth of cell branches and connections within the brain. Much of what young children do as play—singing, drawing, dancing—are natural forms of art. These activities engage all the senses and help wire the brain and create the neural networks needed for successful learning. When children enter school, these art activities need to be continued and enhanced. Cognitive and visual-spatial areas are developed as the child learns songs and rhymes and creates drawings and finger paintings. Dancing and movements during play develop those gross motor skills necessary for survival.

Music can also help young students remember information, such as learning the alphabet through song. Color is also a powerful way to help with remembering information, such as the states of the union and their capitals or the planets in our solar system. The sum of these activities enhances emotional well-being.

The arts also contribute to the education of young children by helping them realize the incredible breadth of human experience around the globe. They begin to recognize the different ways humans express sentiments and convey meaning, and they start to develop subtle and complex forms of thinking (Eisner, 2002b).

The Arts Develop Cognitive Growth

Although the arts are often thought of as separate subjects, like chemistry or algebra, they really are a collection of skills and thought processes that transcend all areas of human engagement. When taught well, the arts develop cognitive competencies that benefit learners in every aspect of their education and prepare them for the demands of the twenty-first century. Elliot Eisner (2002a) of Stanford University identifies these eight competencies:

> **The arts . . . are a collection of skills and thought processes that transcend all areas of human engagement.**

- *The perception of relationships.* Creating a work in music, words, or any other art discipline helps students recognize how parts of a work influence each other and interact. For example, this is the kind of skill that enables an executive to appreciate the way a particular system affects every other subsystem in an organization. This skill also helps a biologist recognize how shifts in one part of an ecosystem can affect several other parts of that system or even other systems as well.

- *An attention to nuance.* The arts teach students that small differences can have large effects. Great amounts of visual reasoning go into decisions about nuance, form, and color to make an art work satisfying. In writing, similarly, great attention to detail in use of language is needed to employ allusion, innuendo, and metaphor. Think how helpful this skill is, for example, to a scientist who is trying to explain a difficult abstract concept to nonscientists.

- *The perspective that problems can have multiple solutions, and questions can have multiple answers.* Good things can be done in different ways. Schools too often emphasize learning focused on a single correct answer. In business and in life, most difficult problems require looking at multiple options with differing priorities and recognizing that each potential solution may have both positive and negative consequences.

- *The ability to shift goals in process.* Work in the arts helps students recognize and pursue goals that were not thought of at the beginning. Too often in schools the relationship of means to ends is oversimplified. Arts help us see that ends can shift in process.

- *The permission to make decisions in the absence of a rule.* Arithmetic has rules and measurable results, but many other things lack that kind of rule-governed specificity. In the absence of rules, it is personal judgment that allows one to assess what feels right and to decide when a task is well done.

- *The use of imagination as the source of content.* Arts enhance the ability to visualize situations and use the mind's eye to determine the appropriateness of a planned action.

- *The acceptance of operating within constraints.* No system, whether linguistic, numerical, visual, or auditory, covers every purpose. Arts give students a chance to use the constraints of a medium to invent ways to exploit those constraints productively.

- *The ability to see the world from an aesthetic perspective.* Arts help students frame the world in fresh ways—like seeing the Golden Gate Bridge from a design or poetic angle.

In the time since Eisner enumerated these competencies, neuroscientists have been developing theories about ways in which art develops cognition.

One common element of the current theories is that each art form involves different brain networks, as shown in Figure 1.4 (Posner, Rothbart, Sheese, & Kieras, 2008). Visual arts are processed mainly in the occipital lobe (the rear part of the brain) and in the temporal lobes (just behind the ears). Linguistic arts (e.g., prose writing and poetry) involve Broca's and Wernicke's areas (the dotted-line ovals)—which are the primary language areas of the brain. Movement arts are processed through the motor cortex, a thin strip across the top of the brain, indicated by the dotted lines. Music is processed by the auditory cortex, located in the temporal lobes.

Using techniques with children that record the brain's electric signals (called electroencephalography or EEG), the researchers discovered that arts training required the children to focus and that this concentrated attention improved cognition. Thus, children who begin participating in arts training at an early age get the benefit of improving their cognitive growth while their brain is still developing. In addition, the arts often involve powerful emotions, and such emotions enhance cognitive processing and long-term memory.

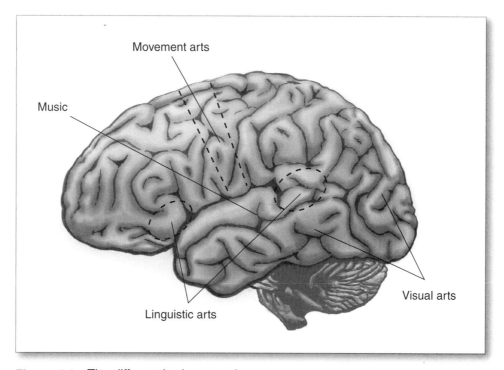

Figure 1.4 The different brain networks.

Source: Adapted from Posner et al. (2008).

At-Risk Students

The impact of arts education can begin as early as preschool. Two studies carried out by the same researchers examined the effects of arts enrichment on school readiness with at-risk preschool students (Brown, Benedett, & Armistead, 2010). The first study looked at achievement within an arts enrichment preschool that served low-income children. These students practiced school readiness skills through early learning of music, creative movement, and visual arts classes. Students who attended the preschool for two years demonstrated higher achievement than those who attended for one year, suggesting that brain maturation alone did not account for the gains in achievement. During the two years that the students attended the program, they were assessed four times. Assessment results continually showed that the students improved in school readiness skills. Furthermore, there were no significant effects of race, ethnicity, or developmental level on the growth of their achievement.

The second study compared students attending the arts enrichment preschool to those attending a nearby alternative school on a measure of receptive vocabulary—one that has been found to predict school success. At the end of just one year of attendance, students in the arts program showed greater receptive vocabulary than those at the comparison preschool.

> *[There is a] strong association between participation in the arts and a wide variety of positive outcomes.*

Perhaps the most impressive study of how arts involvement helped the achievement of at-risk students is the one supported by the National Endowment for the Arts (Catterall, 2012). For the purposes of this study, "at-risk" was defined as those students in the bottom 25 percent of the socioeconomic scale, as measured by their parents' level of education, their employment, and family income. This large study used information from four separate databases, which followed students for a number of years. Three of the databases tracked the students' activities in high school as well as their achievements in early adulthood.

Researchers found a remarkably strong association between participation in the arts and a wide variety of positive outcomes. For instance, students who had rich experiences in the arts during high school showed higher overall grade point averages (GPAs) than did students who did not have those experiences. They even had slightly higher-than-average GPAs in mathematics. Furthermore, the higher grades paid off because the high school students heavily involved in arts-related activities had higher rates of enrollment in competitive colleges—71 percent compared to 48 percent enrollment for their peers who avoided the arts. Not surprisingly, those students in the top 25 percent of the socioeconomic scale also benefited from arts-rich experiences. They had significantly higher GPAs and enrollment rates in colleges than their low- or no-arts peers.

Researchers in this study came to the following noteworthy conclusions:

- Socially and economically disadvantaged children and teenagers who have high levels of arts engagement or arts learning show more positive outcomes in a variety of school-related areas than their low-arts-engaged peers.
- At-risk teenagers or young adults with a history of intensive arts experiences show achievement levels closer to—and in some cases exceeding—the levels shown by the general population in these studies.
- Most of the positive relationships between arts involvement and academic outcomes apply only to at-risk populations (i.e., low socioeconomic status or SES). But positive relationships between arts and civic engagement are noted in the high-SES groups as well.

Of course, these results do not necessarily establish cause and effect. It is possible that the same factors that lead some students toward the arts also make them more likely to excel in other subject areas as well. However, it is also possible that engagement with the arts provides the motivation, stimulation, and satisfaction that have an impact far beyond the arts' classroom.

These findings strongly suggest that an arts enrichment curriculum component may have a positive impact on early brain development and organization, resulting in better educational outcomes for children at risk.

Music

Remember the hype a few years back about music and its ability to raise intelligence—the so-called Mozart effect? What the media failed to report is that the modest boost in test scores for those students who listened to Mozart during the test dissipated after several hours. Nonetheless, the effect raised an interesting question among neuroscientists: In what ways, if any, does music influence the developing brain? Actually, for years researchers have been reporting positive associations between musical experience and cognitive growth in nonmusical areas among young children. But it is important to note that any long-term impact of music on cognitive growth comes from *taking* music lessons over time, which is distinct from the short-term effect of *listening* to music (Schellenberg, 2003). One example of such studies involved more than one hundred second-grade students (Piro & Ortiz, 2009). About half the group studied piano formally in school for three consecutive years. The other half served as the control group and had no exposure to music lessons during that time, either in school or privately. After assessing both groups, the music lesson group had significantly better vocabulary and verbal sequencing scores than did the control group.

Music instruction also appears to help reading by increasing verbal memory—the ability to hold words in temporary memory to complete a thought as one is reading. One study showed that adult musicians had enlarged areas of the brain that are responsible for processing auditory information (Chan, Ho, & Cheung, 1998). Participants in the study with musical training could remember 17 percent more verbal information that those without musical training. The results of a similar study with 90 six- to fifteen-year-old-boys supported these findings (Ho, Cheung, & Chan, 2003). Boys with musical training had significantly better verbal learning and retention abilities. Furthermore, the longer the duration of music training, the better their verbal memory. A follow-up study concluded that the effect was *causal*—that is, the music training caused anatomical changes in the brains of children who were engaged in making music.

Active engagement with music also appears to improve print awareness and writing skills. In one study, children from economically disadvantaged homes participated in instruction that focused on the concepts of print, singing activities, and writing. Participants in the experimental group showed enhanced print concepts and prewriting skills (Standley & Hughes, 1997). Another study replicated this work a few years later with a larger sample of 50 children, and the results again showed significant gains for those students in the music-enhanced instruction in writing skills and print awareness compared to the control group (Register, 2001).

Numerous studies in recent years have shown a strong connection between music and mathematics. For example, one study found that students who had studied a musical instrument prior to fourth grade had higher mathematics scores than those who did not (Haley, 2001). Another study showed that middle school and high school students who were placed in groups with high, moderate, and no music instruction differed in their mathematics achievement (Whitehead, 2001). Those students in the high involvement group showed the greatest gains in mathematics scores.

Music may also have an impact on the young brain by enhancing overall intelligence, as measured by IQ scores. One significant study ran-

> **Research evidence shows a positive connection between music instruction and academic progress.**

domly assigned a large group of children to four different groups—two of which received standard keyboard and voice lessons for a year (Schellenberg, 2004). Of the two control groups, one received instruction in drama, and the other group had no such lessons. All four groups had the expected increases in their IQ scores that are associated with the growth of children at this age. However, the music groups had larger increases in their IQ scores. Participants in the control groups had average increases of 4.3 points, while those in the music groups had increases of 7 points. Furthermore, the two music groups had larger increases than the control groups on all but two of the twelve subtests. In a large study of more than 4,700 elementary and middle school students across four regions of the United States, researchers found a strong relationship between the academic achievement of third and fourth graders (as measured by their test scores) and their participation in high-quality, in-school music programs (Johnson & Memmott, 2006).

Research evidence shows a positive connection between music instruction and academic progress. However, it should be noted that as supportive as these studies on music instruction and achievement may be, we noted earlier that other factors also contribute to this positive effect. For example, factors such as parents who are musicians or who enthusiastically support their child's interest in music, as well as a stable home environment that is conducive to music study, may have an impact on their child's academic progress. Exactly how much of an impact is still not clear.

The Arts Improve Long-Term Memory

Integrating the arts into other content areas, such as STEM, has been shown in numerous studies to improve long-term retention of content. A review of findings conducted by researchers at Johns Hopkins University found that arts integration significantly improved retention of learning through eight effects (Rinne, Gregory, Yarmolinskaya, & Hardiman, 2011). These effects were (1) rehearsing the information and skills, (2) elaborating that adds meaning to the learning, (3) students generating more information, (4) physically acting out the material, (5) students talking about their learning (oral production), (6) the amount of effort that students are contributing to establishing meaning, (7) the degree of emotional arousal over the learning, and (8) representing the learning in pictures.

These findings add to the growing body of solid research from cognitive science and neuroscience about the value that arts-related activities have in helping students remember what they learn. Too often, we hear STEM teachers tell us that their students do not recall much of what they learned in their classes several months earlier. This is an indication that the information never was encoded into long-term memory. Instead, it was retained in the temporary working memory just long enough to take the test, and then it just faded away. We cannot recall what our brain does not possess.

The Arts Promote Creativity

Several definitions of creativity exist, but most seem to include the notion that creativity is, as the saying goes, thinking outside the box. It includes the ability to use divergent thinking to probe deeply and to find alternative solutions to a problem that were not previously considered. Although creativity comes naturally to some individuals, there is growing realization that creativity *can* be taught. It means, however, putting limits on the common instructional approach in today's classrooms that revolves predominantly around convergent thinking—that is, finding the one correct solution to a problem—and where memorization prevails over deep understanding. Schools should be dedicated more to helping students *think* rather than just *know.*

Neuroscientists who are exploring the nature of creativity suggest that creative thinking involves communication among brain regions that do not normally interact with each other during noncreative thinking. Most creative activities involve the brain's frontal lobe; although researchers agree that there is not one single brain area responsible for creativity (Heilman, Nadeau, & Beversdorf, 2003). Brain wave (EEG) and brain-scanning studies reveal that more brain areas are stimulated when performing creative activities than during conventional activities—especially in areas involved in working memory, cognition, and emotion (Chávez-Eakle, Graff-Guerrero, García-Reyna, Vaugier, & Cruz-Fuentes, 2007; Fink, Benedek, Grabner, Staudt, & Neubauer, 2007).

A key revelation regarding the nature of creativity comes from studies using functional magnetic resonance imaging (fMRI) that explored regions of the brain associated with inhibition. One study compared the brain activity of professional jazz pianists as they played the music they memorized to their brain activity as they played spontaneous improvisational jazz (Limb & Braun, 2008). The fMRIs taken during the improvisation revealed that the areas of the brain responsible for inhibition and self-regulation were much less activated than during the memorized performance, but activity increased in the brain areas associated with individuality and self-expression. Apparently, turning off the brain areas that control inhibition and self-regulation leads to less focused attention and spontaneous and creative behavior. Charles Limb, the lead researcher, describes this fascinating study in a video clip available at www.ted.com/talks/charles_limb_your_brain_on_improv.html.

Further evidence of this effect came from a study of six-year-olds (Koutsoupidou & Hargreaves, 2009). Some of these participants had opportunities for musical improvisation during their music lessons.

> *Participation in the arts can foster spontaneity and self-expression, moderate the limiting effects of inhibition, and lead to creative results.*

With others, their music lessons involved more traditional instruction. All students were then assessed with Webster's Measure of Creative Thinking in Music on originality, extensiveness, flexibility, and syntax. Those who were involved with improvisation activities scored significantly higher on the development of creative thinking than those with traditional instruction. Thus, to enhance general creativity in students, the music lessons themselves must involve creative activities. In other words, the best way to be creative is to be creative!

Participation in the arts can foster spontaneity and self-expression, moderate the limiting effects of inhibition, and lead to creative results. It can develop the attentional control for the persistence needed to overcome the fear, frustration, and failure that can accompany creative endeavors. Artistic activities also enhance imaging skills and introspection because they often require one to create and manipulate mental images of a task before doing it and to self-evaluate the quality of one's own performance.

So if creativity is not an innate characteristic that is genetically preset and fixed, how can we teach it? Numerous studies in recent years have focused on this very question, and the results may surprise you. We will discuss those fascinating findings in Chapter 2.

The Arts Advance Social Growth

We live in an age of technology that has transformed the classroom and the nature of instruction. With iPads, laptops, and smartphones, we can be in instantaneous and constant contact with each other. Students walk around tapping their text messages, scrolling on their touch screens, and wearing earphones from morning to night. The average teenager deals with an astounding 3,700 texts a month (Dokoupil, 2012). That is an average of more than 120 messages each day—double the 2007 figure. However, little snippets of online connections through e-mail, Twitter, or Facebook do not substitute for live face-to-face conversation. We have termed this interconnectedness *social media.* But is it? Psychologist Sherry Turkle at MIT contends that this technology is not only changing what we do but who we are (Turkle, 2011). We spend so much time with the technology that there is little time for the experience of developing rich and demanding human relationships. Turkle suggests that we are becoming accustomed to being "alone together," in each other's presence but in our own bubble, connecting electronically but not personally. Perhaps a more appropriate name for "social media" is "antisocial media." We have even observed young people texting each other while seated at the same table!

The recent results of studies in China focusing on the effects of excessive Internet usage on the young brain are disturbing. One study of middle and high school students compared fifty-nine Internet-addicted students with forty-three non-addicted students using an IQ test (Park et al., 2011). The Internet-addicted group had significantly lower scores in comprehension than those of the non-addicted group. Another study found that Internet-addicted adolescents had a lower density of gray matter in the areas of the brain responsible for decision making when compared to non-addicted controls (Zhou et al., 2011). Both studies suggest that Internet addiction may adversely affect the cognitive functioning of adolescents. Furthermore, a long-term study of surveys from about 10,000 children from 2005 to 2009 revealed hardly any increase in parent or teacher attempts to control excessive Internet use (Valcke, De Wever, Van Keer, & Schellens, 2011).

No one questions that the Internet provides valuable opportunities for commerce, political expression, distance learning, and countless sources of information for classroom use. But, regardless of their value, these are impersonal contacts. Humans are innately social animals. We even have regions of the brain that are most active during social interactions and which generate social emotions (Chen, 2009). (Curiously, the great apes, elephants, and other gregarious animals also possess these specialized brain regions.) Having cerebral neurons dedicated to processing social interactions suggests how important social relationships are to human development and behavior. Yet modern technology may be short-circuiting this development by diverting our social interactions to the electronics rather than to face-to-face conversations.

Turkle further suggests that we are becoming more comfortable with technology than with one another. We seem to prefer the illusion of companionship through online connections without the demands of relationships. Here is where experiences in the arts may help. Many activities in the arts require collaboration through group planning, problem solving, and performance. They foster discussion, debate, and teamwork. In the early 1870s, French sculptor Frédéric Bartholdi designed the Statue of Liberty but eventually needed the engineering genius of Gustav Eiffel to design the interior framework to support the statue and its raised arm. The arts may be a major contribution in the STEM curriculum toward counterbalancing the antisocial, anti-collaborative nature of today's technology.

The Arts Introduce Novelty

Teachers remark that capturing students' attention these days is not an easy task. Yet attention is necessary for most learning to occur (Heimann, Tjus, & Strid, 2010). Neuroscientists have been exploring the nature of attention for decades and now seem to agree that it is a complex process involving three separate, integrated neural systems (Figure 1.5). One system is the *alerting* (sometimes called arousal) system that monitors the environment for any unusual (novel) activity or emotion. A teacher who begins lessons the same way every day does not represent unusual activity (and probably neutral emotions) and thus will often not be successful in activating the alerting system. The students' brains are thinking, "Same old, same old . . ." But when the alerting system does detect a novel event, the second system, called the *orienting* system, causes the individual to face toward the source of the alert—in this case, the teacher. Now the brain must make a decision what to do, and that is the job of the third system or the *executive control* area located in the frontal lobe.

When a teacher starts the class by saying, "We're going to do something different today" or "I have a surprise for you," the students realize that

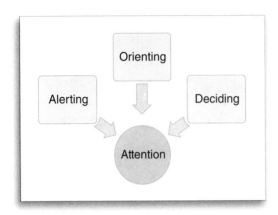

Figure 1.5   These three neural systems are used to get an individual's attention.

something unexpected is about to happen, and their attention rises dramatically. By integrating arts-related activities, teachers offer plenty of opportunities for novelty. Asking the students to draw their answers, put them to song, or act them out is sure to raise the students' interest and participation.

We recognize that some STEM teachers may be resistant to introducing music, dance, and role-playing into their classrooms. Some may think it silly or maybe inappropriate. However, remember that using novelty does *not* mean the teacher needs to be a stand-up comic or the classroom a three-ring circus. It simply means using a varied teaching approach that involves more student activity along with lesson components and emotional stimuli that the students did not expect. Appropriately used, novelty—especially those involving arts-related activities—can add new interest and fun to learning the STEM concepts.

The Arts Reduce Stress

Creating an artistic product can be a pleasurable experience that stimulates the brain's reward system and sends a rush of a chemical called dopamine across neurons. This dopamine torrent gives us a feeling of euphoria and lowers our stress levels. A study in Japan divided 57 healthy college students (27 males and 30 females) into four groups, each of which participated in thirty-minute sessions of one of the following creative activities or a control activity: playing the piano, molding a piece of clay, writing calligraphy, and remaining silent (the control group) (Toyoshima, Fukui, & Kuda, 2011). Before and after each session, the researchers measured the blood levels of the stress hormone cortisol and administered an anxiety inventory to each participant. The post-session cortisol levels were markedly decreased for piano playing, clay molding, and writing calligraphy, indicating a reduction in stress due to participation in these creative activities. Interestingly, the effect of piano playing was significantly greater than clay molding and writing calligraphy. In addition, the post-session scores on the anxiety inventory decreased significantly in all groups except for the control group, indicating a reduction in anxiety induced by engaging in creative activities. In other words, creative activities are valuable mental health tools for reducing anxiety is schools, which are often very stressful environments.

All of these research findings alone should justify teaching the arts for the arts' sake, and one should not have to suggest that we teach the arts only because they enhance the learning of other academic subjects, such as STEM. Nonetheless, it may be necessary to document any spillover effects that learning the arts can have on learning other subjects. That is because of the risk that the arts will fall by the wayside as schools are held more accountable for improving achievement in language arts and mathematics.

> *Arts education is [not] only for those students who want to be artists.*

It is encouraging that more states have recently promoted the arts in their curriculum through policies, such as including the arts as part of high school graduation requirements, standards, and assessments. Although the extent of commitment varies, some states have developed more extensive programs in the arts for schools and created partnerships with state arts councils and local arts organizations. We must be cautious, however, not to accept the notion that arts education is only for those students who want to be artists. To do so would imply that we should teach history only to those students who want to be historians and science only to those who want to be physicists, chemists, or biologists.

The Arts Make Teaching More Interesting for STEM Teachers

A 2011 poll found that only 44 percent of teachers were "very satisfied" with their job (MetLife, 2012). This was the lowest level in the annual poll's 28-year history. Teachers reported that they feel too tied to the curriculum and have little leeway for creative planning and instruction. As they get frustrated, their motivation begins to wane. If they get bored, the students are bored.

More beginning science and mathematics teachers leave the profession after their first year than teachers in other subject areas. A University of Pennsylvania study showed that the first-year dropout rate was 18.2 percent for science teachers, 14.5 percent for mathematics teachers, and 12.3 percent for all other subjects (Ingersoll, Merrill, & May, 2012). Integrating arts-related activities can liven up the curriculum content, make the lesson more successful and interesting to both teachers and students, and introduce much-needed creative thinking into the teaching-learning process. When teachers see success in their classrooms as a result of their efforts, they are more likely to stay.

THE ARTS AND STEM DO HAVE DIFFERENCES

We recognize, of course, that in our zeal to integrate arts and STEM, we need to acknowledge that there are differences between the arts and STEM. For instance, the criteria for deciding what makes good art are quite different from the criteria for deciding what makes good science or good engineering. Another difference is in the generation of ideas and product. Any new idea that a scientist has, say making brackish pond water suitable for drinking, has most likely been thought about and tried by another scientist somewhere else, or would be at some future time. The real world is the ultimate determiner of whether that new idea will work. But think of an artist creating a product, say Leonardo da Vinci painting his *Mona Lisa,* or John Philip Sousa composing "Stars and Stripes Forever," or John Milton writing *Paradise Lost.* If they did not produce those artistic products, nobody else could have. Thus, the idea for an artistic product (such as a painting, song, or poem) is far more linked to the individual artist than a scientific idea is to an individual scientist. Sure, some scientific discoveries are associated with their discoverers, such as Albert Einstein with $E = mc^2$, and James Watson, Rosalind Franklin, and Francis Crick with the DNA helix. However, the point is that other scientists would probably have made these discoveries later because these were areas of intense scientific interest and investigation.

Some critics of STEAM argue that the arts and STEM subjects are very different ways of looking at the world. Although the areas share some communality, the critics are wary that students may not understand the critical differences. This is a legitimate concern. However, we believe that teachers who are aware of how arts and STEM learning intersect and support each other can competently demonstrate to students the important differences in these two domains of human activity. Furthermore, the integration strategies we suggest in the ensuing chapters make these differences clear.

STEM Learning Needs the Arts

Indeed, the arts can enlighten STEM in many ways. Robert Root-Bernstein (1997) offered some vivid examples:

- The elegant shape of Buckminster Fuller's geodesic domes can describe soccer balls and architectural buildings, as well as the structure of viruses and some recently discovered complex and enormous molecules.
- NASA employs artists to design visual displays that present satellite data as accurate, yet understandable to nonscientists.
- A biochemist looks at the fiber folds in her weaving cloth and recognizes another way of explaining protein folding.
- Computer engineers code messages to the frequencies of a specific song to prevent interception or blocking of the message, unless the decoder knows the song.
- Genetic researchers convert complex data into musical notation to facilitate analysis of the data, as, for example, decoding the sequence of genes in a chromosome.

Of course, the two people who probably personify STEAM are the Renaissance figures Leonardo da Vinci and Michelangelo Buonarroti. Although these fierce competitors were known more as painters and sculptors, they were also renowned as inventors, engineers, and scientists. For example, da Vinci conceptualized the helicopter and battle tank and made important discoveries in anatomy, hydrodynamics, and optics. Michelangelo also worked as an architect and engineer, designing the large dome of St. Peter's Basilica in Rome. These men saw no boundaries between the arts and sciences. Their work is inspiring, so let's take a closer look at how arts training can directly relate to the goals of STEM education.

Skills for Learning STEM and the Arts

As we mentioned in the Introduction, the STEM initiative is a logical extension of the framework recently proposed by the National Research Council (NRC) that was designed to address perceived weaknesses in K–12 science education in the United States (NRC, 2012). This proposal will likely become the basis for the next generation of core standards in science. The NRC framework consists of three dimensions: (1) scientific and engineering practices, (2) crosscutting concepts, and (3) disciplinary core ideas. This last dimension identifies specific content for the physical, life, earth, and space sciences, as well as for engineering, technology, and the applications of science. So let's set that one aside and focus on the first two dimensions, which deal with learning certain skills and broad concepts. Our premise here—based on recent research findings—is that students who have been exposed to arts-related instruction will have an advantage in acquiring these STEM-related skills and concepts over students who have not.

To support our premise, Table 1.2 lists in the left column the practices and concepts from the first two dimensions of the NRC framework. Alongside in the right column, we have listed some of the cognitive, emotional, and physical skills that students can acquire as a result of participating in arts-related instruction. As the arrow in the table indicates, the interaction works in both directions. Just as arts-related skills can enhance the learning of STEM concepts, so can the introduction of STEM concepts into standalone arts courses help those students understand the nature, development, and application of artistic skills.

Playing the piano, writing a poem, acting out a role, performing a dance, or creating a painting sharpens observations, hones details, stimulates multiple brain networks, and puts things into context. These are the same tools needed by a good scientist, mathematician, or engineer. The study of the arts not only allows students to develop skills that will improve the quality of their lives but also sustains the same creative base from which scientists and engineers seek to develop their innovations and breakthroughs of the future. In Chapters 4, 5, and 6, we explore in greater detail how integrating arts-related skills supports STEM learning at various grade levels.

Table 1.2   Practices and concepts from the K–12 National Research Council framework and skills often acquired in arts-related instruction.

First Two Dimensions of National Research Council Framework	Skills Acquired in Arts-Related Instruction
Scientific and Engineering Practices:	*Instrumental and Vocal Music, Art, and Dance Instruction:*
1. Asking questions and defining problems	1. Exploring the various ways to create art and make an informed decision
2. Developing and using models	2. Researching and appreciating the work of other artists, such as an analysis of a Beethoven sonata
3. Planning and carrying out investigations	3. Making color choices for a mural based on other works, as well as applying understanding of color and color variations.
4. Analyzing and interpreting data	4. Researching a written work, such as *Romeo and Juliet,* and creating a ballet interpreting the work
5. Using mathematics and computational thinking	5. Creating a series of pottery measuring cups, calculating the amount of clay, and the amount of kiln-shrinkage to have exact proportions
6. Constructing explanations and designing solutions	6. Writing a script based on a current events issue
7. Engaging in argument from evidence	7. Having a team create a comic strip in a roundtable format, based on a current political situation
8. Obtaining, evaluating, and communicating information	8. Creating a puppet show based on the "greenhouse theories."

(Continued)

Table 1.2 (Continued)	
Crosscutting Concepts:	
1. Patterns	1. Discussing and performing rhythmic and melodic musical patterns
2. Cause and effect; mechanism and explanation	2. Experimenting with different media in creating a work of art on paper: watercolor vs. acrylics vs. chalk vs. pencil
3. Scale, proportion, and quantity	3. Creating a sculpture
4. Systems and system models	4. Analyzing the orchestration of a symphony both by visual review of the score and listening cues
5. Energy and matter: Flows, cycles, and conservation	5. Choreographing a piece depicting reclamation of western Pennsylvania steel mill buildings and land
6. Structure and function	6. Creating a set for a stage production
7. Stability and change	7. Analyzing and listening to the history of jazz in America

Source: Adapted from National Research Council (2012).

WHAT'S COMING?

In this chapter, we have looked at *why* we believe it is advantageous to integrate arts-related skills into STEM instruction and to use STEM concepts to enhance learning in the arts. In the next chapter, we explore what researchers in neuroscience and cognitive psychology are discovering about the brain and learning as it relates to the arts, STEM, and creativity. It will address theories about how we think, examines how mind-set has such a powerful influence over student achievement and teacher success, and delves into the nature of creativity. Be prepared for some fascinating revelations.

Chapter 1—Why STEM Should Become STEAM

Major Points to Ponder

Jot down key points, ideas, strategies, and resources that you want to consider later.

_____

_____

_____

_____

_____

_____

_____

_____

_____

_____

_____

_____

_____

Chapter 2

What Science Says About the Arts and Creativity

The mere formulation of a problem is far more often essential than its solution, which may be merely a matter of mathematical or experimental skill. To raise new questions, new possibilities, to regard old problems from a new angle, requires creative imagination and marks real advances in science.

—Albert Einstein

In the United States, the No Child Left Behind Act (NCLB) introduced a requirement that new educational programs be subject to rigorous scientifically based research that proves they are effective. Despite persistent criticism that the NCLB has stifled creativity and innovation in school, this requirement was a novel idea because many programs in schools were adopted based on anecdotal records or just plain hunches. Of course, schools are not chemistry or physics laboratories where variables can be carefully controlled. Nonetheless, there are research protocols that do allow for the testing of programs and interventions in schools using experimental and control groups of students, similar to an approach used in medicine. Another aspect of scientifically based research, as defined by the U.S. Department of Education, is that it "employs systematic, empirical methods that draw on observations or experimentation." This is where the findings from research in cognitive psychology and educational neuroscience come in.

In this chapter, we look at some of those research findings that have implications for teaching and learning. Specifically, we take a look at how we believe the brain is organized for learning and thinking. Doing so will help us better understand how arts-related skills and STEM skills can work together to enhance the acquisition and retention of learning. This information can be very useful because it provides the scientific basis for supporting arts integration and gives you the ammunition you need to defend your instructional choices. We also explore the nature of creativity and what scientists are discovering about this important mental talent.

BRAIN ORGANIZATION

We have often heard people refer to scientists, mathematicians, and engineers as very logical, analytic, and precise individuals. On the other hand, they refer to people in the arts as creative, holistic, and visual. These descriptions are largely the results of lingering stereotypes. Obviously, scientists can be creative and artists can be logical. Further support for these stereotypes comes from the misinterpretation of some research regarding the functions of the brain's hemispheres that led to a popular notion of "left-brained" and "right-brained" people. This is a good time to clarify what scientific research has revealed and to distinguish between myth and experimental findings.

The human brain is divided into two main hemispheres that are connected by a thick cable of nerves called the *corpus callosum* (see Figure 2.1). This cable allows information to travel between the hemispheres so that the individual gets the benefit of whole-brain participation and integration. Conventional thought in recent years is that the two hemispheres perform somewhat different tasks during information processing. This concept is the result of watching what happens to the thinking and learning processes of a person with a particular type of brain damage. For example, damage to the left front part of the brain frequently results in spoken language problems, indicating that this must be a brain area specializing in the processing of spoken language,

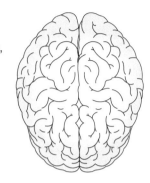

Left Side:

Literal interpretation of language

Recognizes words, letters, and numbers written as words

Analyzes for details

Detects time and sequence

Performs arithmetic calculations

Processes joy

Right Side:

Contextual language

Recognizes faces, places, and objects

Does spatial perception

Highly active during creative processing

Does relational mathematics like geometry and trigonometry

Processes sadness and depression

Figure 2.1   The left and right hemispheres are specialized and process information differently. However, in complex tasks, both hemispheres are engaged and communicate through the corpus callosum, a bundle of nerves that connects the halves.

especially vocabulary. Follow-up studies with brain-imaging techniques have confirmed the existence of some of these specialized regions.

It seems our left brain monitors the areas for speech in most right-handed people. A few left-handed people have their speech centers in the right hemisphere (Duffau, Leroy, & Gatignol, 2008). The left hemisphere understands the literal interpretation of words and recognizes words, letters, and numbers written as words (Ellis, Ansorge, & Lavidor, 2007). It is analytical, evaluates factual material in a rational way, perceives the detail in visual processing, and detects time and sequence. It also performs simple arithmetic computations (Zamarian, Ischebeck, & Delazer, 2009). Arousing attention to deal with outside stimuli is another specialty of the left hemisphere, and it appears to process positive emotions such as joy (Hecht, 2010).

Meanwhile, our right brain gathers information more from images than from words and looks for visual patterns. It interprets language through context—body language,

There is no neuroscientific evidence to support the notion that one hemisphere consistently dominates a person's thinking, learning, or behavior.

emotional content, and tone of voice—rather than through literal meanings (Campbell, 2006). It specializes in spatial perception; recognizes places, faces, and objects; and focuses on relational and mathematical operations, such as geometry and trigonometry. It is highly active when people are engaged in creative tasks. This hemisphere also appears to process negative emotions, such as sadness and depression (Hecht, 2010).

A Note of Caution

As interesting as this hemisphere specialization is, the question that remains is whether this has any influence on how we learn and how we view the world. Since the research on brain specialization was first published several decades ago, popular media, infomercials, and even stand-up comedians commented on whether people were mainly "left-brained"—that is, analytical, logical, and sequential, or "right-brained," meaning holistic, artistic, and creative. Although many individuals exhibit these combinations of abilities that may be *perceived* as being primarily left- or right-brained, there is no neuroscientific evidence to support the notion that one hemisphere *consistently* dominates a person's thinking, learning, or behavior. Anatomically, the corpus callosum connecting the two hemispheres facilitates communication between them. Our environment is constantly bombarding us with vast amounts of information—so much so that our brain needs to process it in two separate ways simultaneously! Fortunately, the hemispheres work together when dealing with most tasks, thus giving us a more complete picture of what is happening around us and helping us decide whether or how to respond.

THINKING AND LEARNING

Essentially, arts integration is an instructional approach in which the elementary-grade or subject-area (STEM) teacher uses the arts to help students to construct meaning and demonstrate understanding in *both* the particular art form and another subject area, thereby meeting specific learning objectives in both. Learning can take place through any artistic medium that uses creativity as a means of making authentic connections with the knowledge, skills, and processes of another subject area. As a result of these connections, the students have a deeper understanding of both the art form and the STEM concepts. This deeper understanding should meet specific and significant learning objectives that can be measured through various forms of assessment. To understand ways in which arts-related activities can expand student thinking in STEM, let's take a look at the major types of thinking that we ask students to do during instruction.

Convergent and Divergent Thinking

One way to describe types of thinking is to separate them into convergent and divergent processes (see Figure 2.2). In convergent thinking, the student brings together material from various sources that are helpful in solving a problem at hand. The material generally includes piecing together relevant facts, data, and procedures that allow the student to arrive at the single correct answer. Convergent thinking works best with well-defined problems that have definite responses. This approach is usually appropriate in the STEM areas when we solve for the value of x, determine the molecular weight of a chemical compound, calculate the wavelength of a particular frequency, or the torque of an engine. Furthermore, this is generally the only type of thinking that is measured in standardized tests because there is only one answer, making it easy to machine grade while reinforcing the need for test reliability and consistency. In convergent thinking activities, for example, the student does the following:

- Uses litmus paper to decide which liquids are acids, bases, or neutral (Science)
- Solves for the value of x in the equation, $5x + 17 = 52$ (Mathematics)
- Determines which of three different bridge models can safely carry the most weight (Engineering/Technology)

In some STEM classrooms, the students are completing experiments that merely confirm a scientific principle that they have already learned. Such an activity is of little interest and hardly challenging. Furthermore, student thinking does not move very far up the levels of Bloom's Taxonomy (see Chapter 9).

In divergent thinking, on the other hand, the student generates several ideas about possible ways to solve a problem, often by breaking it down into its components and looking for new insights into the problem. After gaining those insights, the student may then use convergent thinking to put the parts back together and solve the problem in a different and unexpected way. For example, after using divergent thinking to create different melodies and harmonies, the composer then needs to use convergent thinking to put that

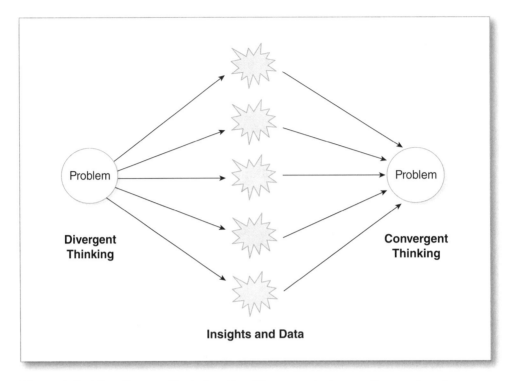

Figure 2.2 The diagram illustrates the differences between divergent and convergent thinking.

music to paper, using strict rules of musical notation, so that other musicians can correctly play the composition. Divergent thinking works best with poorly defined problems that have multifaceted solutions. This is the type of thinking that is typical of artistic activities. Measuring a student's divergent thinking requires asking open-ended questions such as these:

- Think of as many uses as you can for each of the following: a paper clip, a blanket, a brick.
- In what other plausible ways could Shakespeare have ended *Romeo and Juliet*?
- If you saw a creature from another planet, how would you communicate to it that you meant it no harm?
- What criteria would you use to determine if an artistic painting is of high quality?

The mental processing involved in divergent thinking moves students to higher levels of complex thinking. The actual time that teachers devote to divergent thinking in STEM classes is often limited because the STEM areas—as currently taught in our schools—lend themselves so well to convergent thinking, and because testing STEM concepts is easier with closed-ended questions that have only one correct answer. Yet this type of instruction may be extinguishing creativity in our students. Some researchers believe that by consistently reinforcing neural pathways with convergent thinking activities, we may be limiting the pathways that support creative and divergent thinking (Kraft, 2007). There are many opportunities for open-ended questions in STEM areas if teachers are willing to plan for them. For example, teachers could ask students to do the following:

- Think of as many principles of physics/chemistry/biology you could investigate using each of the following: a paper clip, a blanket, a brick.
- What common household objects could you use to make pond water drinkable?
- What criteria would you use to select the most aesthetic of several different (and safe) bridge designs?

These types of questions require the brain to search through numerous neural networks for any stored ideas, pieces of data, and frameworks that can help create possible solutions to the problem. Thus, divergent thinking drives the creative process, activating more parts of the brain than convergent thinking and making new neural connections. Using *both* forms of thinking challenges the brain to use its maximum capabilities to get a deep and comprehensive understanding of the problem and its potential solutions.

We recognize, of course, that some teachers prefer more conventional approaches to teaching STEM concepts. Some STEM area teachers have even expressed to us skepticism over whether the extra time they would need to incorporate more divergent thinking activities—whether arts-related or not—is worth the effort. This is important because studies find that a teacher's mind-set about student behavior while learning can actually enhance or hinder creativity in his or her classroom (Beghetto, 2006). When a teacher demonstrates that creativity is valued, then students will value it as well and be more willing to take creative risks.

Divergent Thinking *Challenges* the Brain—That's a Good Thing!

Because divergent thinking requires the brain to analyze information and assess options, it activates more cerebral networks than ordinary problem solving. One way to determine this scientifically is to measure brain waves (electroencephalography, or EEG) while an individual is performing tasks requiring convergent and divergent thinking. Several EEG studies have shown higher brain wave activity during divergent thinking than during convergent thinking (e.g., see Jauk, Benedek, & Neubauer, 2012). Higher activity suggests that the divergent tasks are more challenging, and the brain responds by recruiting more neurons in order to determine how to accomplish the task. This involvement of additional neural regions allows the brain to make new connections between different and distant networks, both within and between the cerebral hemispheres. The expanding association of neural pathways increases the brain's ability to find new patterns and to manage more complex and challenging problems in the future. Imaging studies confirm that individuals with more extensive neural connections demonstrate greater creativity than those with fewer connections (Takeuchi et al., 2010).

A simple example is a study of the solar system. One author visited a middle school science class that was studying the solar system. There were data sheets around the classroom with information about each planet's size, distance from the sun, surface temperature, and possible atmospheric composition. The students were asked to pick two planets, learn their specific characteristics, and share them orally with the class. This lesson met the curriculum objectives but was hardly exciting or creative.

In a similar situation at another middle school, the teacher asked students to review the basic characteristics of each planet, just as in the first scenario. But then she moved the students into divergent thinking. She asked the students to pick one planet and draw a picture of what a living creature on that planet might look like, given the gravity, atmospheric, and other conditions on the planet. They would then explain why they chose that shaped creature to the class. She also asked them to explain what kind of protection a human astronaut would need to survive on their chosen planet. Finally, if they could rename the planet, what name would they choose that they believe would more accurately describe it.

Divergent Thinking *Changes* the Brain—That's a Better Thing!

Imaging techniques used by cognitive neuroscientists revealed in the 1990s that divergent thinking activated numerous areas of the brain, especially the prefrontal cortex (see Figure 1.2). You will recall that this is the area where creativity and decision making occurs. But does divergent thinking actually change brain structure? Apparently, yes. The first real evidence of that came from the study of musicians. For example, one brain imaging study of thirty professional musicians found that the corpus callosum was significantly larger than a matched group of nonmusicians (Schlaug, Jäncke, Huang, Staiger, & Steinmetz, 1995). Recall that the corpus callosum is the thick cable that connects to the brain's two hemispheres and allows communication between them. However, these results left unanswered this classic question: "Which came first, the chicken or the egg?" Was the increase in brain structure size the result of musical practice or were these individuals born with a larger corpus callosum that predisposed them to pursue music?

The answer to the "chicken-or-egg" question came a few years later with a now-famous study of taxi drivers conducted by researchers at the University College in London (Maguire et al., 2000). Why taxi drivers? Candidates for a taxi license must undergo extensive training to learn the names and locations of thousands of London streets. This training takes an average of two years. In essence, the candidates create a mental map of the city and the best routes for driving around efficiently. Such knowledge requires considerable use of spatial navigation, a skill thought to have an impact on brain structure.

Researchers aimed their imaging devices at the part of the brain called the *hippocampus.* Located deep in the emotional brain, one of its roles is to facilitate spatial navigation and memory. (The hippocampus helps you remember the best route for driving to work as well as the alternate routes when the best one is blocked.) The hippocampi of the taxi drivers were significantly larger than those of a control group. Furthermore, the volume of the hippocampus correlated with the years of experience as a taxi driver: the longer one drove the taxi, the larger the volume of the hippocampus. Here was research evidence of the brain's plasticity—its remarkable ability to alter its structure in response to environmental demands.

Further evidence of the brain's plasticity and musical training came from a study of six-year-old children who had no prior musical training (Hyde et al., 2009). One group consisted of fifteen children who received weekly, half-hour private keyboard lessons for fifteen months. The matched control group consisted of sixteen children who did not receive any instrumental music training during the fifteen-month period. However, they did participate in a weekly forty-minute music class consisting of singing and playing with drums and bells. Brain imaging revealed that the children in the keyboard group had increased brain size in the corpus callosum and in the frontal lobe, and they demonstrated increased motor and auditory processing skills, when compared to the control group. This research evidence strongly suggests that, at the very least, artistic endeavors that involve developing spatial navigation and learning instrumental music enhance the growth of brain structures in children and adults.

Why Don't Schools Engage in More Divergent Thinking?

Most students have experienced a school culture that is focused mainly on "getting the right answer and getting it quickly." Their in-class and standardized testing formats reinforce this approach to learning. They have had few opportunities past the primary grades to practice divergent thinking. After all, divergent activities generally take more time and are more demanding and time-consuming to evaluate. Frankly, many teachers themselves admit that they have not had a lot of experience or training working with divergent strategies (Andiliou & Murphy, 2010; Kampylis, Berki, & Saariluoma, 2009). Consequently, most classroom teachers ask their students for focused attention to a whiteboard and to absorb information. In other words, the current classroom is not designed to encourage divergent thinking or creativity.

> **The current classroom is not designed to encourage divergent thinking or creativity.**

On those few occasions when students are challenged with a divergent task, they balk due to their lack of familiarity with this type of challenge. They quickly recognize that trying to solve the problem will take much more effort and time. Add to this situation another critically important factor called mind-set, one of the greatest *barriers* to student achievement and creativity.

Mind-Set: It Can Hinder or Improve Achievement

Mind-sets are those beliefs, assumptions, and expectations that guide how we behave and how we interact with others. These mind-sets start forming at an early age as we grow and interact with our parents, friends, and elements of our culture. Our brain stores summaries of those interactions in cerebral networks. New experiences strengthen and expand these networks. Eventually, they become so ingrained that we react almost reflexively when those similar situations arise again. For example, when we spot a dear friend, neural circuits fire in the emotional and motor areas of the brain causing us to spontaneously smile, extend our arms, and show warmth when we meet. On the other hand, different circuits fire in the presence of a demanding boss or bully, causing us to stiffen and display deference or anxiety.

Researchers who study mind-set suggest that at a young age we develop either a fixed or a growth mind-set about the origins of our ability and success (Dweck, 2006). Those who develop a fixed mind-set accept the premise that we are born either smart or not smart, either able or not able (see Figure 2.3). Although environments can contribute a bit to our ability, the genetic predisposition to be a good scientist or a poor one, a great base-ball player or a mediocre one is so strong that it will determine whether an individual will do well in a given pursuit. A person with a fixed mind-set believes that the main predictor of success is *ability.*

By contrast, people who develop a growth (or fluid) mind-set operate from a fundamentally different perspective on ability and success. Growth–mind-set individuals believe that although genetics might frame a starting point in our development, it is really one's own determination and persis-tence that predicts success. A person with a growth mind-set believes that the main predictor of success is *effort.*

Most researchers believe that people are born with a growth mind-set. The human brain is designed to collect information from its environment and consolidate it so it can begin to make those decisions needed to keep its owner alive. Think of our ancestors on the African savannah. Many of the

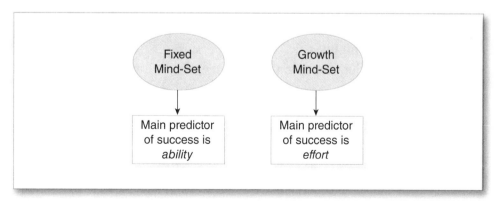

Figure 2.3   Fixed mind-sets focus on ability, while growth mind-sets focus on effort.

decisions they faced involved solving problems with more than one answer. Which path through the jungle is the safest? How do I avoid encountering animal predators or hostile tribes? What type of prey am I more likely to catch for food during the rainy season, and what is the best way to trap them? Individuals with superior divergent thinking skills and a growth mind-set were far more likely to survive than those without such skills and thus pass their genes on to their offspring.

This growth approach is evident in toddlers as they explore their toys and their world and work at trying to make sense out of it. So if you accept that we are born with a growth mind-set, why is it that so many school children display a fixed mind-set? What happens between birth and the early school years to cause this drastic change? Clearly, the attitudes and beliefs of the child's parents or caregivers continually convey both overt and subtle messages about ability that alter the mind-set as the child internalizes them. Teachers, too, can convey these messages—sometimes not so subtly.

Because mind-set is such a powerful and ingrained force, it is not surprising for students who hear they are "not smart" to see themselves that way, while students who hear that they *are* smart to see themselves that way as well. "Not smart" students attribute their lack of success to factors beyond their control, making statements such as, "Nobody in my family is good at science or math" or "I just don't have any talent as a musician." Often the result is that these students give up in the face of difficulty—such as in a divergent thinking activity—because they believe the ability to do the work is simply not in them.

> *Even highly able students can suffer as well in a class where teachers put a premium on being smart rather than on working hard.*

Ironically, even highly able students can suffer as well in a class where teachers put a premium on being smart rather than on working hard. These students conclude that smart is something they were born with. When they encounter work they cannot easily accomplish, it indicates that they are not smart after all, because smart people do not have to work hard and this task would require serious work. Often, then, the student will reject the challenge. In fact, bright students with a fixed mind-set will often select easier tasks within a class and opt to take easier classes. They reject feedback on their work as negative judgment and work for grades rather than for the sake of learning, because it is the grade that signals smartness and success.

Teachers with a growth mind-set believe that most students can learn most things if they will exert the necessary effort. Students working with growth–mind-set teachers recognize that they should celebrate effort, not genetics, and that they can have an impact on their own success. They develop a sense of self-efficacy as learners and are more likely than fixed–mind-set peers to learn for the sake of learning, to persist in the face of difficulty, and to see feedback as a mechanism for continued improvement. Developing a growth mind-set is important to both teacher and student success.

Changing One's Mind-Set in STEM and the Arts

Students with a fixed mind-set in STEM areas will be reluctant to attempt challenging activities because of fear of failure, especially if they have a teacher with a fixed mind-set. Yet there is ample research evidence to show that, thanks to the brain's plasticity, teachers and students can change their mind-set from fixed to growth when in an environment that is challenging, rewarding, and motivating (Dweck, 2006). This is more likely to happen in classrooms where the following occurs (Sousa & Tomlinson, 2011):

- A teacher connects with each student and indicates a belief in that student's value and potential.
- Each student in the class must have consistent responsibilities for successful operation of the class.
- Students learn to work with increasing independence and self-awareness as learners.
- Students need to be partners in the belief that every student in the class can and will succeed with the most essential content.
- A major goal for the classroom is students competing against themselves rather than against one another. That is, student growth is an expectation for success.
- The teacher plans for challenging the high-end students and differentiates instruction to support virtually all students in achieving those goals.
- All students work at tasks that are equally interesting, appealing, and important—all of which require high levels of reasoning.

Interest in Music and Art Increases in High School

A review of the previously given elements shows that a key force in

Several studies have found that high school students who get involved with arts-related activities are more motivated to go to school and less likely to drop out.

changing from a fixed to growth mind-set is motivation. A student's motivation to learn various subjects in school varies with the student's personal interests, such as hobbies and sports, as well as the student's age. A recent study of more than 3,000 students in Grades 6 through 12 showed that their interest in science and mathematics, which was high in middle school, dropped significantly as these students moved from middle school to high school (McPherson & Hendricks, 2010). However, their interest in music and art, which was low in middle school, increased significantly in high school. Several studies have found that high school students who get involved with arts-related activities are more motivated to go to school and less likely to drop out (e.g., Ramey, 2005). These findings suggest that incorporating arts-related activities in STEM subjects are likely to stir students' interest and increase their motivation to learn and thus stay in school.

THE ARTS, STEM, AND CREATIVITY

What is creativity? There are dozens of books on the market that deal with creativity as seen from each author's perspective. Although there are significant differences among the authors' views of creativity, there is general consensus about a few points. To be sure, it is not a single entity but rather a collection of different thought processes. At the very least, creativity involves divergent thinking, insight, and a product. However, creativity is more than just thinking about and producing something novel. The product must have value and be accepted in the domain of knowledge that it affects. It is not just generating alternatives to solving a problem; it is the *uniqueness* and *feasibility* of those alternatives. There is a difference between creativity and fantasy. Fantasy disconnects us from the real world and envisions actions that could never happen in reality. Creativity has a purpose: to solve a problem or produce a product. It often comes from connecting old ideas that seem to have no relation to one another in a new way.

Creativity Versus Intelligence

In Chapter 9, we discuss some of the theories on intelligence, and most researchers agree that intelligence is related to creativity but that there are differences. Psychologists look at intelligence broadly as involving problem-solving skills and as a mental trait that is measureable by a series of tests that yield an IQ. Individuals with above average IQ often attain high levels of success, but a much smaller number of them become successful artists, writers, composers, innovative scientists, actors, or musicians. It seems that highly creative people tend to have above average intelligence, but lots of people with above average intelligence are not very creative. This observation lends support to the notion that creativity is a separate brain capability from intelligence.

Stages of Creative Thinking

The creative process is generally well summarized by French mathematician Jacques Hadamard who wrote that it consisted of four stages (Hadamard, 1954). Although he proposed these stages more than a half century ago, the findings from today's studies in neuroscience support much of his work. Here are his stages (see Figure 2.4) and what current research is revealing:

- *Preparation:* This is a period of intense conscious attention to the task that continues until our thinking processes reach an impasse and we are stumped. It seems the harder we focus on trying to find the insight, the more likely that discovery will not happen. That's because the more we focus on something, the more information is sent to working memory, located just behind the forehead. Working memory is where we consciously process information and our ideas. But it has a limited capacity, and when it gets overcrowded, the processing begins to stall. At this point, we realize that we need to take a break, to give working memory an opportunity to clear out the clutter.
- *Incubation:* This is a period of relaxation away from the task. The brain may look at the problem with new perspectives or simply daydream. We once believed that brain activity quieted down during daydreaming. But scanning studies now reveal that this is a time when the brain is highly active. Suddenly, parts of the brain that do not normally directly interact start messaging each other (Snyder & Raichle, 2012). Researchers believe that because the brain is not responding to outside stimuli during this down time, it can turn its attention to browsing

internal networks and making remote associations. This provides us opportunities for literally creating new connections and for seeing inferences and patterns that we may have previously overlooked. And then . . .

- *Illumination:* The "aha" moment occurs—that time when the solution or insight suddenly becomes clear. Some researchers suggest they have actually detected when this powerful insight moment will happen. Using EEG, they have detected a rush of brain waves in the right hemisphere of individuals up to eight seconds before their insight actually occurred (Sandkühler & Bhattacharya, 2008).
- *Verification:* This occurs when we carry out all the tedious work necessary to see if the solution will actually work. Here is where more convergent thinking may be needed to gather the necessary resources to implement the solution.

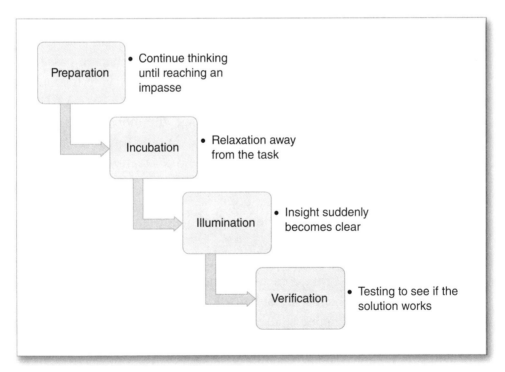

Figure 2.4   These stages represent one way of examining the creative process.

Source: Adapted from Hadamard (1954).

There are two surprising findings from this current research on the creative process. The first is the realization that the more focused we become

> *Insights are more prone to come to us when we are relaxed, such as going for a quiet walk or taking a warm shower.*

on solving the task, the more difficult it is to do so. This result runs counter to our long-standing belief that the more undivided attention we devote to solving a problem, the more likely it will come to us. It seems that is not the case—mainly because we are too fixated on processing the information *outside* our head. The second surprise is the finding that insights are more prone to come to us when we are relaxed, such as going for a quiet walk or taking a warm shower. These tranquil activities allow our brain to play around with what is *inside* our head, making those connections that lead to the "eureka!" moment. Of course, this tranquil time will be difficult to provide in any classroom where the teacher feels compelled to keep moving in order to "cover the packed curriculum."

Everyone Can Be Creative

Until just a few years ago, many psychologists believed that creativity was a fixed trait—either you had it or you didn't. But in recent years, scientists have found that creativity is part of human nature—hardwired into all of our brains. Just carrying on a conversation with someone is a creative enterprise. Your brain must sift through tens of thousands of stored words, select the ones you need to express your thoughts, and string them together according to the rules of grammar and syntax so that you can be understood—all in fractions of a second. Of course, like intelligence, creativity is not equally distributed in the population; some people are more creative than others. Physician and researcher Nancy Andreasen (2005) uses the terms *ordinary creativity* to describe what most of us possess and *extraordinary creativity* for those we consider geniuses, such as Einstein, Michelangelo, and Mozart. But we all possess creativity to some degree, and the great news is that we can get better at it. How did researchers discover this? Actually, this idea that we all can be creative emerged from evidence involving several different areas of scientific research.

One set of research studies involves working with patients who have an unfortunate medical condition that results in the deterioration of the brain's frontal and temporal lobe areas. Called *frontotemporal dementia,* this fatal disease slowly eats away at the prefrontal cortex. You may recall from Chapter 1 that this area controls the brain's executive functions and restrains our impulses. Doctors working with some of these patients noticed that, even as their executive functions declined, they began to take an intense interest in creative art projects, such as painting, sculpturing, and drawing (Seeley et al., 2008). Puzzled at first, the researchers finally realized what was happening. As the disease destroys neurons in the prefrontal cortex, the brain's ability to control impulses is weakened, and those flourishes of creative thought from the right hemisphere are unleashed. The patient can enjoy several years of artistic productivity before the disease takes it ultimate toll.

A second set of studies involves sleeping and dreaming. For instance, one study asked participants to translate a string of digits using two simple rules that allowed the string to be reduced to a single digit (Wagner, Gais, Haider, Verleger, & Born, 2004). The researchers built a hidden rule into the strings that, when discovered, would make the task much easier. Only about 20 percent of the participants could find the hidden rule. However, during the retest of three groups of participants (those who slept, those who stayed awake during the day, and those who stayed awake during the night), nearly 60 percent of the participants who got eight hours of sleep gained the insight to discover the hidden rule. Why did this happen? As we sleep and dream, our prefrontal cortex releases the brain to make spontaneous and unrestricted associations among ideas—associations that would not be allowed while we are awake and the prefrontal cortex is exerting its control. Many of the random associations made during our dreams could never happen in the real world, but sometimes an association actually leads to insights that will help us solve a real problem when we awaken.

Creativity in the History of Science

The history of science reveals several occasions when discoverers credited dreams for resolving issues they were pursuing. There is the German organic chemist August Kekulé who had been attempting for years to uncover the molecular structure of benzene. He admitted in his writings to falling asleep in a chair by the fireplace in 1865 when visions of snakes danced in his head. One of the snakes grabbed hold of its own tail, and when Kekulé awoke, he realized that benzene had a circular structure, not a linear one like the other organic compounds known at the time. Inventor Elias Howe is said to have gotten the idea for the sewing machine in 1845 after awakening from a dream in which he was captured by cannibals who kept pushing him into a pot with spears that had holes at the tip, not at the end as with handheld sewing needles. Albert Einstein recalled a dream he had in the late 1890s where he was sliding down a hill in a sled that kept increasing his speed. As the sled approached the speed of light, he saw the stars refracted into colors. When he awoke, he realized the dream had importance for his thoughts about mass and the speed of light, which ultimately led to $E = mc^2$.

Given all this evidence about creativity, why do children begin to resist creative activities as they move from the primary to the intermediate elementary grades? Science writer Jonah Lehrer notes that 95 percent of second graders say they are creative—they like to paint and draw and to

> *Fear of making an error suppresses their creativity. . . . [The students'] experience in school has been that making an error almost always results in a penalty.*

think up stories. In fifth grade, that number drops to 50 percent. Regrettably, only 10 percent of high school seniors see themselves as creative (Lehrer, 2012b). What accounts for this rapid decline in these students' self-assessment of their creativity? Are schools that proficient at discouraging creativity? Have students internalized the myth that creativity is a rare gift?

No doubt there are multiple reasons. Here is one biological explanation. The emotional brain is fully functional by ten to twelve years of age. However, the prefrontal cortex is slow to develop and does not mature until around the age of twenty-two to twenty-four years. In the primary grades, the prefrontal cortex barely censors their activities. These students create with abandon and for the pleasure of it. But as they move into the intermediate grades, their prefrontal cortex is developed enough to start exerting its inhibiting effects. Students begin to worry about how their teachers and peers view them. What if they say the wrong thing, sing the wrong notes, or draw the wrong picture? Fear of making an error suppresses their creativity. Furthermore, their experience in school has been that making an error almost always results in a penalty of some sort.

Creativity in STEM Areas

The standard view of professionals who work in STEM areas as cold, detached individuals governed mainly by facts and empirical data may fit some. But many great discoveries in STEM have been made by those individuals using creative thought processes that linked old ideas to form new ones. We have all heard the stories of Archimedes in the bathtub recognizing the principle of buoyancy and how Isaac Newton's observation of an apple falling from a tree led to this theory of gravity. Here are a few more examples:

- Johannes Gutenberg used his understanding about wine presses to make the first movable-type printing press in Europe. (Moveable type and crude presses were being used in China and Korea several centuries earlier.)
- Alexander Fleming noticed that a mold growing in a bacteria culture he accidentally left uncovered in his laboratory had destroyed the bacteria around it, resulting in the discovery of penicillin.
- The Wright brothers did not create the first airplane but used their experience working with bicycles and motors to produce the first stabilized flying aircraft.
- When Percy LeBaron Spencer walked past an operating radar tube at the Raytheon Company, he noticed that the chocolate bar in his pocket had melted. He then put some popcorn in front of the tube and it popped all over the room, leading him to develop the microwave oven.
- After a walk in the Swiss woods, George de Mestral noticed burrs sticking to his clothes and his dog's fur. He examined how they were attached and invented Velcro.
- Arthur Fry thought to apply a seemingly useless weak adhesive developed by a colleague to a piece of paper for a bookmark so it would not damage the book, and the Post-It note was born.

Each of these individuals had a flash of insight that took old ideas to new and unexpected levels. Insight is a component of creativity, and it turns out that we have a part of the brain that gets highly active when we have an insight (Jung-Beeman et al., 2004). Called the anterior superior temporal gyrus, it is located in the right hemisphere just behind the right ear (see Figure 2.5). Earlier studies had shown that this area responded dramatically when the brain was processing jokes and abstract literary devices, such as metaphors and subtle story plots. Researchers proposed that these language skills were related to insight because they require the brain to make distant connections between seemingly unrelated ideas.

Why don't these examples of creativity get portrayed in science classrooms? Why does the notion that the STEM areas are more logical and far

less creative than the arts persist, and why do so few high
school students—presumably
including those in STEM
classes—think of themselves
as creative? We suggest two
reasons: First, because of the
vast amount of material to be
covered, most STEM concepts
taught in K–12 classes involve
a lot of memorization, minimal
real-world experimentation,
and mostly convergent thinking. There are few exposures
to creative problem solving in
these classes or to the stories
of creative successes in STEM.
As one well-meaning high
school science teacher noted,

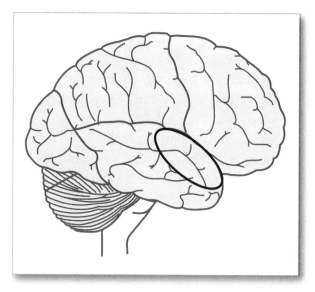

Figure 2.5   The neurons that respond to insight,
a critical component of creativity, reside in the
anterior superior temporal gyrus, just behind the
right ear (indicated by the oval).

"I just have too much to cover in the curriculum to get involved in time-
consuming, far-out ideas." Second, few if any arts-related skills are integrated into STEM classes. As a result, STEM students do not perceive these
subject areas as requiring creative thought, and these perceptions will stay
with the students as they become adults. The clear message is that we need
to include more creative activities in STEM classes, and the arts provide an
ideal and motivating way to do so.

STEM Professionals in the Real World

Researchers looking into STEM classrooms often report that many of
these courses lack any of the features that characterize what STEM
professionals do in the real world (Yager, 2007). For example, at the mid-
elementary through high school grades, teachers concentrate so much on
delivering textbook information that they fail to develop in students a curiosity about the STEM concepts and events or possible explanations for
them. The students' practice in STEM classes usually involves carrying
out experiments or solving problems where the outcomes are already
known—hardly a challenge or incentive to be creative. They do not have

the opportunity to collect evidence to establish the validity of their *own* explanations of STEM problems or to communicate those explanations and their evidence to others. Furthermore, the STEM curricula assume that students must know what previous scientists and mathematicians have produced before they can experience real-world science and mathematics on their own. Consequently, K–12 students spend thirteen years trying to learn what others report about the natural world without having much occasion to create their own questions and seek out possible answers.

Once teachers believe that they *can* plan their STEM to generate creativity in their students, amazing things happen. In one study, twelve middle school science teachers (Grades 6–9) were trained in how to use higher-level, challenging questions in one class and a traditional, teacher-dominated, lecture-type lessons in another class of matched students (Yager, 2007). During an eighteen-week period, both classes had pretests and post-tests on identical content. The graph in Figure 2.6 shows the dramatic results in the percentage of students demonstrating creative-thinking skills in both types of classes. The students in the creative sections were able to apply their learning in new situations. However, those in the traditional-approach classes remembered what the teacher had taught, but they were unable to apply their knowledge in new situations. In other words, there was no transfer of learning.

Without transfer to new situations, any STEM learning is of limited value. For instance, in a 2009 National Assessment of Educational Progress test of *performance* in science experiments, 71 percent of the 2,000 fourth graders tested could accurately choose how volume changes when ice melts, but only 15 percent could explain *why* that happened, using evidence from experimental data (National Center for Education Statistics, 2012). Throughout the test, fourth, eighth, and twelfth graders could accurately report what was happening in science scenarios with limited data, but they could not manipulate variables or make decisions as part of conducting the experiment. Only a small number of students were able to justify or explain their answers based on the experimental findings. In sum, students were able to memorize the facts and report data but could not explain them. Whatever instruction these students experienced in their science classes obviously did not foster scientific thinking. Rather, it encouraged rote memorization with little or no understanding of the scientific principles involved. Do we keep doing what we are doing? Or do we look for innovative ways to make the learning of science a joyful and meaningful experience?

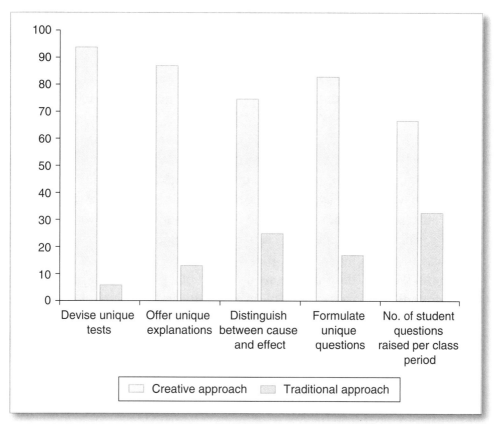

Figure 2.6 The percentage of students able to use creative thinking skills in classes using a creative thinking approach and the traditional thinking approach.

Source: Adapted from Yager (2007).

The question now is to determine what types of experiences can persuade students to be creative in STEM classes and how arts-related activities can be the motivating force behind those experiences. Here is an example using a typical experiment that would be done in a general science classroom (Barrow, 2010). The experiment involves asking the following research question:

How does the number of ice cubes affect the temperature of water?

The traditional procedure is to take a measured amount of tap water and determine how much the temperature changes in degrees Celsius as ice cubes are added. The students already learned that the temperature will fall, and the task is simply to measure the new temperature with the addition of more ice cubes.

> **When students act alone and submit their report for a grade, a competitive, rather than a collaborative, atmosphere prevails.**

Each student performs the experiment alone, completes a fill-in-the-blank report, and submits it to the teacher who grades it and eventually moves on to the next topic. When a student acts alone and submits his or her report for a grade, a competitive, rather than a collaborative, atmosphere prevails. As contrived as this description may appear, the authors have seen this kind of approach on numerous occasions. It does not represent what scientists and engineers do in the real world.

How can we make this experiment more challenging and interesting using arts-related skills? One skill that many artists have to develop is collaboration. Whether they are staging a concert or a play, writing and producing a musical composition, singing in a chorus, or dancing in an ensemble, these artists have to work with others to make their creative product a success. In this experiment, rather than students working individually, they could work in groups of three to four students to create new questions of inquiry. (A group of more than four gives some students an opportunity to observe or disengage rather than actively participate.) Another skill essential for arts-related activities is visualization. How will this product *look* if we are successful? A third skill is brainstorming to provoke new ideas about variables that could affect the outcome of the product. Another powerful arts-related skill is feedback, that constant assessment by one's self and others to determine whether and what types of actions would improve the product. So, for example, using these skills the group (collaboration) does the following:

- Draws the various shapes that ice cubes come in (visualization), and determines if shape makes a difference in the rate and number of degrees the temperature changes when added to the tap water. Examples are cube, crushed, half moon, cylinder, etc.
- Discusses (brainstorms) other variables and comes up with varying: the initial amount of water (50 ml, 100 ml, 150 ml, etc.), the starting temperature (10°C, 15°C, 20°C, etc.), the time intervals between temperature measurements (one, two, three minutes, etc.), the composition of the container (e.g., plastic, Styrofoam, glass, metal), the type of water (e.g., tap, bottled, distilled), and the size of the glass container (graduated cylinder of 25 ml, 50 ml, 100 ml, etc.). The variables would

be divided among the students in the group who would then pool their results with the other group members.

- After collecting and analyzing their data, each group reports its results and conclusions to the rest of the class for review and discussion (feedback).

The arts-integrated activities in this scenario have support from cognitive neuroscience. First of all, the students are working in groups and

> *By talking and sharing ideas, [students] are more likely to process and remember what they have learned.*

talking about the learning objective, so synergy (the idea that the whole is greater than the sum of its parts) is at work. Thoughts are fermenting and colliding until a new idea emerges. Simply put, more heads are better than one. Second, the students are talking to each other, and we know that talk is one of the most powerful memory retention devices there is. By talking and sharing ideas, they are more likely to process and remember what they have learned. Third, reporting and explaining their findings to the rest of the class allows for cognitive rehearsal—another effective strategy for retention. Fourth, the feedback from their peers gives them opportunities to review their findings to determine if their experimentation was appropriate and accurate.

Figure 2.7 summarizes the two approaches. Which do you think is more interesting and challenging for the students? Granted, the arts-integrated approach might take a little longer. But it is a wise investment of time. The tasks of collaboration, visualization, brainstorming, and feedback will all greatly increase the likelihood that the learning will be remembered—certainly a desirable goal. Furthermore, compared to the traditional approach, the students will get a far more accurate view of what scientific inquiry is really about, and these are all *transferable* skills.

Does Technology Foster Creativity?

Now that technology is firmly entrenched at all grade levels in today's classrooms, can we assume that students will now be more creative in their STEM classes? That depends on how the technology is used. In some classrooms, the technology is used simply for doing the *same* things faster rather than for engaging students in *different* things. With this scenario, technology

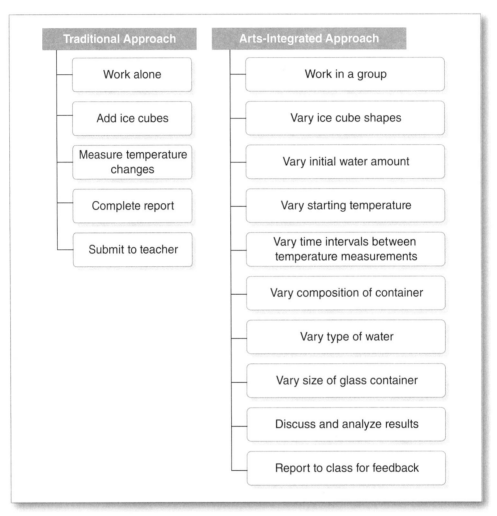

Traditional Approach	Arts-Integrated Approach
Work alone	Work in a group
Add ice cubes	Vary ice cube shapes
Measure temperature changes	Vary initial water amount
Complete report	Vary starting temperature
Submit to teacher	Vary time intervals between temperature measurements
	Vary composition of container
	Vary type of water
	Vary size of glass container
	Discuss and analyze results
	Report to class for feedback

Figure 2.7 Comparison of the traditional and arts-related approaches when carrying out a science experiment. Which one do you think will be more motivating and challenging for the students?

is a means for increasing instructional efficiency. It becomes a tool for "covering the material" faster in a teacher-dominated environment where student interest can lag and attention can drift. Sitting students at their own separate computer to master STEM content at their own pace is certainly better than a teacher lecturing during the entire learning episode, but does it foster creativity? Probably not. Where is the novelty in this approach?

Instead, use technology and arts integration to make learning easier for the teacher and so much more intriguing for the students. Using their own creativity, teachers can show students how technology helps them pursue their interests, merge arts-related activities with their STEM learning, collaborate and help each other achieve the instructional objectives, communicate with arts and STEM experts around the world, and become more responsible for their own learning and achievement. Technology can help students examine real-world problems, complete STEAM projects, and learn to think and write like a STEM apprentice.

Some STEM and other subject-area teachers view technology as a potential threat to their job. As technology becomes more sophisticated, perhaps schools will need fewer teachers. That concern is understandable but unwarranted. Good teachers cannot be replaced by machines. The Gallup organization has spent decades studying what makes a great classroom teacher (Bushaw & Lopez, 2011). They find that these three basic traits consistently emerge in successful teachers:

- They know how to develop productive relationships with their students, colleagues, and parents.
- They are energetic and know how to inspire students with their own enthusiasm for their subject.
- They really get to know each student, they treat each one as an individual, and they select individualized tasks that will help that student succeed.

Successful teachers engage their students emotionally as well as intellectually, and arts-related activities can provide that emotional component so that a so-so STEM class becomes an exciting and creative STEAM class.

WHAT'S COMING?

We recognize that before teachers are willing to consider attempting arts integration, they have a number of essential questions that need to be answered. What do you mean by the arts? How do I work with a real artist? What if I am not very artistic? How can I provide time in my busy schedule? What about the Common Core State Standards (CCSS)? The next chapter answers these important questions.

Chapter 2—What Science Says About the Arts and Creativity

Major Points to Ponder

Jot down key points, ideas, strategies, and resources that you want to consider later.

_____

_____

_____

_____

_____

_____

_____

_____

_____

_____

_____

_____

Chapter 3

Frequently Asked Questions About Integrating the Arts and STEM

 Creativity is allowing yourself to make mistakes. Art is knowing which ones to keep.

—Scott Adams,
American cartoonist and writer

Integrating arts-related skills and activities with STEM concepts can be done by investing a little time up front to organize curriculum and instruction for the integration; we will explain this in the following chapters. Every school and teaching situation is as different as the children we teach, and understanding that is a concept that is often lost with the proposed implementation of a new program. What an author or clinician proposes simply might not work for you in your specific circumstance. In this chapter, we will start by clarifying what we mean by the "arts." Then we will address a number of frequently asked questions (FAQs) as well as define parts of the process in order to make moving from STEM to STEAM an enriching and enjoyable ride for you and your students.

WHAT ARE THE ARTS?

What a loaded question! The complete answer is certainly a long one, and with the increasing use of technology in the arts, there are creative possibilities that do not even yet have names. For the sake of the many activities in this book, we are including the forms of artistic expression listed below. And, of course, the beauty of all of this is that one form can, and often does, cross-pollinate with another form, such as in a mixed media painting.

> **With the increasing use of technology in the arts, there are creative possibilities that do not even yet have names.**

MUSIC

- Choral/Vocal
  - Vocal technique
  - Performance
  - Choral technique
  - Composition
- Instrumental
  - Solo instrument
  - Orchestra
  - Marching band
  - Composition
  - Ensemble
  - Concert band
  - Jazz ensemble
- Music appreciation
- Computer-generated music

ART

- Drawing
  - Pencil
  - Markers
  - Charcoal
  - Crayon
  - Chalk
  - Cartooning

- Painting
  - Acrylic
  - Oil
  - Watercolor
- Pottery (including mosaics)
- Sculpture
- Fabric art
  - Quilting
  - Painted fabric
- Murals
  - Painted
  - Found objects
- Paper
  - Making paper
  - Origami
- Art appreciation
- Computer-generated art

DANCE

- Dance instruction
  - Ballet
  - Jazz
  - Modern
  - Tap
  - International/Ethnic
- Choreography
- Production
- Dance appreciation

DRAMA/THEATER

- Drama and acting classes
- Speech and vocal production
- Mime
- Productions of plays and musicals
- Original and adapted scripts
- Drama/Theater appreciation
- Theater technology
  - Theater lighting design and operation
  - Audio/Sound design and operation
  - Set design and construction
  - Costume design and construction

- Puppetry art
  - Design and creation of puppets
  - Design and creation of puppet stages

FILM

- Film production
  - Film editing
  - Video
  - Creating soundtracks and special effects
- Different genres
- Anime/Animation
- Film appreciation

CREATIVE WRITING

- Writing in different genres
- Readings
  - Poetry slams
  - Coffee houses
  - Rap
- Listening/Appreciation
- Technology
  - Translation

ARCHITECTURE, GARDENING, AND LANDSCAPE DESIGN

- Basic design
  - Traditional
  - Computer generated (CAD)
- Plant origins and species
- Materials
- Understanding local growing conditions
- Design of community and school gardens
- Appreciation
- Preservation issues

Keep in mind that all these art forms can be used in collaborative projects with students in other countries via the Internet.

ADDRESSING SOME COMMON FREQUENTLY ASKED QUESTIONS

We recognize, of course, that teachers and artists who are exploring the possibility of trying arts integration in schools often have some very important questions that need to be addressed. These questions reflect concerns that center on whether teachers need to have extensive training in the arts, or how much time it will consume in an already crowded school day, or whether it will affect students' test scores. Here are our answers to these questions, recognizing that they may not be applicable to every situation.

Question 1: How Can I Do This if I Am Not an Artist and I Am Not Creative?

One of the most common responses we get from teachers at all grade levels is that they do not think of themselves as artistic in any way, and the very thought of having to create art, something beyond "coloring" in the classroom, can be very intimidating. We hear stories where teachers were told as children, "Please don't sing, dear," implying that the person was a poor singer or did not experience any kind of formal musical or artistic training. Students were told to color or draw "within the lines," not allowing for any freedom of expression and making them fear that going outside the lines was wrong—the antithesis of the process that we know activates the problem-solving regions of the brain. As well-intentioned as these directives were, they actually had the reverse effect: They put a damper on creative expression.

Even if you have rarely had the experience of attending live musical, theatrical, or dance performances or of viewing art in a museum or gallery, don't worry. Every day you make

> *Every day you make artistic choices in one way or another.*

artistic choices in one way or another: You change the channels on your television, you select the music you listen to at home or in your car, as well as make decisions about the colors and fabrics that you wear and that surround you in your home. Creative decisions are a daily part of your life. Now, let's ensure that creative decisions are part of the students' experience in our schools.

We approach STEAM with the understanding that all of us have some sort of artistic talents within ourselves and that some of these talents are simply more developed than others. It is amazing how many classroom teachers who, as children, studied dance, took a few years of piano or instrumental music lessons, spent hours creating model cities from Legos, found fabric pieces and other items to create puppets or make kites, loved drawing things (yes, chalk on the sidewalk does count), or uttered the classic line "Let's put on a show" and family and friends were invited to attend the "Broadway performance" in the backyard.

Now is the time to pause to think about what kind of art and music pleases you and why. Reflect on the arts experiences you have had in your life, and bring all of this to the forefront. As you implement STEAM, you just might find the Picasso, Balanchine, or even Lady Gaga buried deep inside. Take the risk! In doing so, you practice what you preach, and you will inherently allow your students to begin to take the same risks as they travel down the road of learning authentic problem solving, a necessary skill to fully understand what STEM professionals do and how they do it. At the end of this chapter is a self-assessment called the "Arts Perception Worksheet." It will give you some thought-provoking insights on how you look at the arts.

Question 2: What About Arts Integration Versus Art for Arts' Sake?

If you are a movie-goer, then you know that MGM Studio's logo shown at the beginning of every MGM movie is a roaring lion's head poking through a circle of film. On the film is the phrase "Ars Gratia Artis," which is Latin for "Art for the sake of art." This book is designed to assist educators in the use of the arts as an instructional tool in the delivery of the core competencies for courses in science, technology, engineering, and mathematics. By no means are we implying that the arts need to affect how well a student learns a STEM subject as measured by standardized tests in order for the arts to exist or to have purpose in a school or after school. After all, the arts have arguably been a part of human life long before the STEM areas emerged.

Ideally, schools should be institutions of learning

> *[The arts] foster inter- and intrapersonal experiences that break down social and cultural barriers.*

where choral and instrumental music, dance, art, and drama have equal weight on their own in the curriculum. Youth participating in the chorus, playing in the orchestra, or painting a mural and then rushing to basketball practice creates a cultured institution, nurturing the best in all youth. The results of such programming are almost impossible to measure, but we know it when we see it, and we feel it when we hear it.

These experiences foster inter- and intrapersonal experiences that break down social and cultural barriers. The communal experience of working and learning together in many settings fosters friendships and deeper understandings of different cultural and ethnic backgrounds and the acceptance of the ways other people think. It sets the stage for meaningful learning to happen. It is an indomitable part of a liberal arts education that is endangered in schools nationwide. Unfortunately, high-stakes testing and the trend toward specialized schools, even at the elementary-grade level, steals the uplifting experience of children being exposed to the various learning opportunities that can enrich their lives.

The goal is to have a school where these activities and programs happily coexist, the school administration promotes healthy collaboration between arts and the academic teachers and extracurricular instructors (sports, etc.), and where they help each other in the delivery of quality curriculum. For example, a reading teacher can learn much from a choral music teacher, who is usually teaching vocabulary well above a student's grade level through the lyrics in a piece of choral music. Conversely, a choral teacher can learn much from a reading teacher regarding how students learn sentence structure, grammar, hyphenation, and story sequence.

Question 3: Is There a Difference Between an Artist and a Teaching Artist? artist in residence

Some of the suggestions we will make in the following chapters include bringing into the classroom local professional artists who will use their expertise to enhance the STEM concepts. Ideally, these artists would visit on a regular basis and establish a working relationship with the school district. In addition to carrying out the necessary legal checks on the artists, the district should also develop a training program to ensure that the artists' time in the classroom will be productive.

We recognize that such a program has to be compatible with existing local and state regulations and with teacher contracts. The question of whether the

> **Teaching is an art as well as a science.**

teaching artists get a stipend needs to be addressed. Some districts have received outside grants to cover the cost of the stipends. Despite these potential hurdles, a number of school districts have successfully implemented this type of program (see, for example, the Center for Creative Education [CCE] project in the Resources section at the end of this book).

Of course, care must be taken in selecting the candidates for teaching artists. Just because a person might be an excellent pianist, painter, dancer, or actor does not mean that the person has the ability to teach. Teaching is an art as well as a science. An artist, with no training in pedagogy, needs to learn how to teach. As in any other profession, there are a few people who have an innate ability to do something very well with little or no training. Often you hear "She was born to teach," or "He was born to sing." Most often, that is not the case. Teaching and singing are skills that require extensive practice to perform them well.

In the 1980s, the St. Augustine School of the Arts in the South Bronx created a unique situation where academic teachers and teaching artists worked side-by-side on a daily basis. This necessitated the training of teachers to be artists and artists to be teachers. Over the years, many other organizations, such as the Chicago Arts Partnerships in Education, have done the same. Unfortunately, the training of teachers at the undergraduate and graduate level in the United States has not changed much for well over fifty years, save for a few institutions that have taken the risk and have created truly innovative approaches to teaching. Our dream is that new and unique instructional strategies such as arts integration would become a staple at these institutions nationwide, but that topic is outside the scope of this book.

The training of artists to become teaching artists is a challenging yet extremely creative process. As with any instructional strategy, this process is actually a model for what should take place in the classroom. The CCE in West Palm Beach, Florida, has been training teaching artists since 1999. The challenge for this training program is to never dilute the artistic integrity of the artists and their work but to work with the artist to develop effective teaching skills and strategies as well as an understanding of mandated state standards. The format in Figure 3.1 describes a typical year of training for a teaching artist. Note that the training includes exposure to the Theory of

Multiple Intelligences and Bloom's Taxonomy of the Cognitive Domain. You will find detailed explanations of these models in Chapter 9. There are, thankfully, many schools that have music, dance, art, and drama teachers. You should work with these colleagues, and if they are great teachers themselves, they will become a tremendous resource for you. As you will see later in this book, there are numerous ways to collaborate with these artists and teachers of the arts, and all of you will be glad that you did.

**TEACHING ARTIST PROFESSIONAL DEVELOPMENT
PART A—Each session is three hours.**

- Multiple Intelligences—Putting theory into practice
- Bloom's Taxonomy—Understanding the relationship to the artistic process
- Classroom management
- Creating effective lesson plans and time management
- Understanding state standards and grade-level expectations
- Working effectively with special needs children
- Teaching in a multi-language and multicultural classroom
- Temperament and teaching—Making practical use of your Myers-Briggs' personality type in the classroom
- School law issues—Understanding your responsibilities and the responsibilities of the site/school staff where you are teaching
- Collaborating with a teacher, after-school practitioner, or another teaching artist—A facilitated discussion with teachers, after-school practitioners, and other teaching artists about what is necessary for authentic collaboration for successful delivery of programming

**TEACHING ARTIST PROFESSIONAL DEVELOPMENT
PART B—Practicum**

- Observations (4)—Observations of four different experienced teaching artists in the classroom of after-school venue
- Mentor-Partner teaching (2)—Partnering with an experienced teaching artist in presenting a prepared lesson
- Immersion day—A culminating, full-day of professional development with focus of the creation of sample lesson plans, teaching parts of the plan to other attendees for verbal feedback, and review of all of the professional development topics in Part A
- Teaching artists assessment—An ongoing process where teaching artists are assessed by appropriate staff as well as teaching artists doing self-assessment and assessment of their particular sites

---

Figure 3.1   This is an outline of the professional development training for a teaching artist used by the Center for Creative Education in West Palm Beach, Florida.

Way too often, these teachers do not always get the respect they deserve, and they become important only when it is time for a holiday show or a special presentation. They too often teach in a vacuum imposed by scheduling, time constraints, and by their physical location in a school. A school that has a music or an art teacher who roves from room to room unfortunately sends a message to everyone that music and art are just not that important to deserve rooms of their own. These teachers can be a gold mine of valuable information and ideas for you. Befriend them, take them to dinner, and then plan your work!

Question 4: Can a STEM Teacher Think Like an Artist and an Artist Think Like a STEM Teacher?

We acknowledge that trying to adapt STEM lessons to incorporate arts-related activities means taking risks. Too often, teachers, especially at the elementary school level, are told exactly what to teach and when. This micro-management approach can suck all of the creativity out of a teacher. Working with the arts and artists, on the other hand, can unleash a teacher's creativity while providing exciting and challenging experiences for the students.

Imagine, for example, working with a professional potter who uses her art not only as a means for a student to create an amazing and beautiful piece of pottery but also to reinforce concepts in mathematics (see Figure 3.2). The student will have to actively engage in measurement when creating the initial drawing for the piece, thus using both visual and spatial intelli-

> *Creating arts-integrated lesson plans innately promotes a collaborative culture within the schools.*

gences. Measurements and estimations for the amount of clay and kiln time will need to be made to determine the size of the finished work, requiring logical and mathematical intelligences. It is also clear that the inter- and intrapersonal intelligences will be blanketing the entire process, creating the motivation for the student to know, understand, and apply mathematical operations. A STEM teacher who can see that the arts open creative ways to deliver curriculum is in for an amazing experience. As we have already noted, the arts not only activate the brain in many ways but they also help to create learning environments that are supportive, enriching, and happy. The concept of collaborative learning has been around for a long time (remember the Socratic Method?). When it first hit classrooms in the 1970s, it was new ground for teachers who taught children sitting alone at their desks, seldom if ever talking with fellow students about their learning. However, collaborative learning was nothing new for choral, instrumental, and dance teachers. That was always the very basis of how they taught, and the finished product was most often a collaborative effort.

Creating arts-integrated lesson plans innately promotes a collaborative culture within the schools and classroom and certainly between the teacher and a teaching artist. A valuable sidebar to this experience is that the students observe two adults working together—sometimes disagreeing yet always coming up with the *best* answer. The transference of such positive interaction is probably impossible to accurately assess, but we can feel it, see it, and almost touch it. And coming up with the best answer is often contrary to "teaching to the test," a situation that, unfortunately, is the mantra for many schools. Teachers who use alternative instructional methods, such as arts integration, bring a level of richness to the learning experience for the student, to say nothing of the enriching experience for the teachers themselves. As you will see later in this book, using the arts as an instructional tool can produce the same instructional outcomes while enriching the experience for everyone.

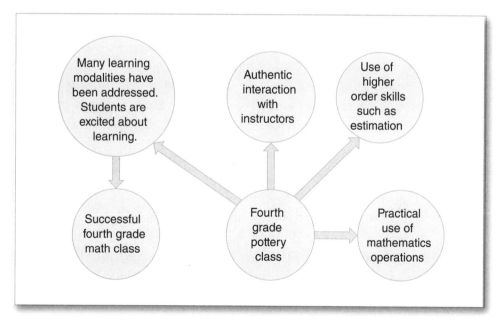

Figure 3.2   This pottery lesson engages students to use STEM concepts.

Question 5: How Do I Make My Schedule Provide for Arts Integration?

We initially called this section "Creating Time Out of No Time," which sounds poetically lyrical—the words to a song, perhaps. But creating time is, of course, impossible except for an effective teacher. Teachers are continually playing multiple roles every day: educator, mentor, caregiver, and often janitor. Our goal here is to dispel the myth that arts integration is a burdensome add-on and that it will take too much time from the planned day's instruction. This is where it comes down to your outlook and our ability to convince you otherwise.

As with any worthwhile educational strategy, there is an initial amount of time needed to learn and feel comfortable with the new concept and how to implement it. With arts integration, there is usually no need to spend many hours sitting in lectures and reading periodicals and documents about the topic. There is, however, a definite need for the teacher to believe that this is a valid instructional tool, and that comes from knowing the research supporting arts integration—much of which is offered in Chapters 1 and 2 (see Figure 3.3). The other need is for authentic collaboration with an excellent teaching artist and working on a lesson plan together. This activity essentially replaces the traditional professional development format. Even if you do not have the opportunity for this collaboration, there are many suggestions in this book for arts-integrated lesson plans as well as many online resources (see the Resources section).

Whether your collaboration is with an in-person artist or online with other arts resources, recognize that you are experimenting with new ways to deliver the same content that you have been delivering. Perhaps you have actually implemented some of the suggested strategies on your own.

Getting Forgiveness Rather Than Permission

Our experience is that, even today, many teachers are working in elementary and middle schools that do not readily support arts integration or anything else that seemingly takes time away from the core areas of literacy and numeracy or any other content area that is the object of high-stakes testing, an unsettling sign to say the least. On the other hand, if you have a visionary and risk-taking administration, go for it. For those of you who do not, consider doing the following:

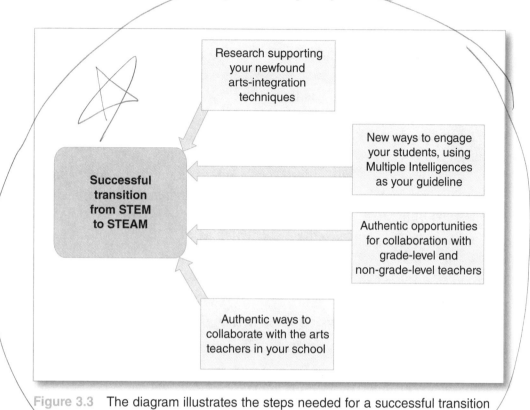

Figure 3.3   The diagram illustrates the steps needed for a successful transition from STEM to STEAM.

1. Create the case for arts integration with school administrators, citing the brain research contained in this book as well as in others listed in the Resources section.

2. Begin creating arts-integrated lesson plans and instructional strategies, finding time to collaborate with other teachers who might be interested.

Question 6: Will Adding the Arts to STEM Affect My Students' Test Scores?

It seems that this is the first question that is asked about anything that comes into a school whether it be a new program or activity or a change in schedule. Research about how the brain learns coupled with excellent lesson planning and informed instruction by dedicated teachers is the key to any kind of learning. Arts integration is no exception. There are some significant issues, however, in measuring the success of arts-integrated instruction. Standardized testing does not tell us *how* a child learned a specific concept, nor does it tell us the thought processes a student used to arrive at an answer. It simply tells us if the answer is correct or incorrect. What we do know from the numerous studies discussed in Chapter 1 is that most students who have arts as part of their school experiences are repeatedly more successful in standardized testing than those who do not. Although we have to be cautious not to automatically assume a cause-and-effect relationship, the data are compelling.

The data aside, it is difficult to deny that when you walk into a room where thirty students are actively engaged in a meaningful creative activity that is supporting content learning, cerebral sparks are flying. New neural networks are being constructed and expanded as excitement, collaboration, exploration, high risk, and success enrich the teaching and learning process. Such experiences result in successful learning and test scores will reflect this.

Question 7: What About Common Core State Standards? Curriculum? Textbook?

Policy makers hope that the Common Core State Standards (CCSS) will produce new and better curricula, but that remains to be seen. A recent study by the Brookings Institution of state standards that have been in effect for years showed that they have had little impact on student achievement (Loveless, 2012). Based on past data, the study predicts that the CCSS will also have little impact on student test scores, despite all the money and effort devoted to this initiative. Why? Because, CCSS lead to an *intended* curriculum, the *real* curriculum has been—and always will be—what happens in the classroom. Written curriculum that is prepared by the state, province, or a local district has all good intent, but it cannot predict the many variations that exist in a school, or even in the same classroom. Variations among the students' native languages, cultures, and cognitive and physical abilities present an everyday challenge to teachers who need to continually monitor and adjust their instructional content and strategies.

Successful schools rely on *authentic* curriculum, which is a local document that is created by the teachers at a particular school and revised about every five years. Authentic curriculum is created based on the following:

> **Successful schools rely on authentic curriculum.**

- National and state standards
- Local (district) directives
- The student population of the school district

This is not to say that a curriculum is a "dumbing down" of national expectations. It means asking the question, "What should every fifth grader know when they graduate from Happy Farms Middle School?" and "What should every twelfth grader know, understand, and be able to do when graduating from this high school?" When those expectations are stated and then aligned with standards, the faculty and staff work together to help all students achieve. Teachers need to consider all their options to make this happen. We propose that integrating arts-related activities are options that can help more students succeed, especially in the STEM areas.

Here is an example of a second-grade STEAM-type lesson in biology (planting a seedling garden) that has been used successfully in schools. It incorporates mathematics (measuring the garden plots), engineering (designing the layout), technology (getting information from the Internet on best plants to use), and the arts-related activities related to visualization. At the same time, the lesson addresses state standards in several curriculum areas. (In this example, we have used the Florida state standards for second grade. They are similar to many other state standards at this grade level.)

Sample STEAM-Type Lesson—Second-Grade Science

Visual Arts Project

Lesson Plan Concept: "The Inch-By-Inch Garden"—Students create a layout plan for their individual indoor seedling gardens made from milk carton bases by measuring the actual carton planting area, cutting out different shapes that are color-coded to represent different flowers or vegetables, manipulating the shapes on blank paper in an outline that they have drawn to represent the area of the planting space, and making decisions on how to use the space and what plants they want to grow. Students collaboratively create their seedling gardens with a partner, measuring and drawing the seedlings as they grow and journaling the entire process.

(Continued)

(Continued)

Mathematics

Benchmarks: (MA.2.G.3.1) Estimate and use standard units, including inches and centimeters, to partition and measure lengths of objects. (MA.2.A.2.1) Recall basic addition and related subtraction facts. (MA.2.G.3.4) Estimate, select an appropriate tool, measure, and/or compute lengths to solve problems. (MA.2.G.5.1) Use geometric models to demonstrate the relationships between wholes and their parts as a foundation to fractions.

Cognitive Complexity: **Moderate to high**

Additional Content Areas Addressed

Science: (SC.2.N.1.2) Compare the observations made by different groups using the same tools. (9SC.2.L.16.1) Observe and describe major stages in the life cycles of plants and animals. (SC.2.E.6.3) Classify soil types based on color, texture (size of particles), the ability to retain water, and the ability to support the growth of plants.

Cognitive Complexity: **Moderate to high.**

Visual Arts: (VA.2.C.2.1) Use appropriate decision-making skills to meet intended artistic objectives. (VA.2.S.1.1) Experiment with tools and techniques as part of art-making process. (VA.2.0.1.1) Employ structural elements of art and organizational principles of design in personal work to develop awareness of the creative process.

Cognitive Complexity: **Moderate to high**

Multiple Intelligences Included

Logical-Mathematical	Linguistic	Intrapersonal
Spatial	Interpersonal	Naturalist

Bloom's Taxonomy
Students move up and down the levels of the taxonomy in this activity, depending on their degree of collaboration and the creativity they use to plan and construct the garden.

Source: Adapted from Florida Department of Education (n.d.).

Sample STEAM-Type Lesson—Fifth-Grade Mathematics

Dance/Bodily-Kinesthetic Project

Lesson Plan Concept: "Dancing Out of This World"—Students study the solar system and learn about the characteristics of the sun, planets, moons, asteroids, and comets and their placement in our galaxy, the Milky Way. After an initial introduction to the material, the students, working in teams, choose one of these topics to investigate further, journaling their research as well as drawing and cutting and pasting photos of their planet or object. Together, the teams choose music that they will move and dance to. Each team will create costume pieces that can be added to every day clothes as simply or as elaborately as conditions permit depicting the color, size, and other special markings of their planet or object. (Creating a constellation would be amazing.) Since these objects are located in the Milky Way, the Milky Way team creates movement/dance to describe the enormity of the Milky Way, and they ultimately surround the classroom. The teams decide how these bodies move around the sun and inside of the Milky Way and create movement/dances to depict this phenomenon. In doing so, they will be collaborative, learn the attributes of their respective planets and stars, and learn to move to specific musical cues.

Science

Benchmarks: (SC.5.E.5.1) Recognize that a galaxy consists of gas, dust, and many stars, including any objects orbiting the stars. Identify our home galaxy as the Milky Way. (SC.5.E.5.2) Recognize the major characteristics of all planets and compare/contrast the properties of inner and outer planets. (SC.5.E.5.3) Distinguish among the following objects of the solar system—sun, planets, moons, asteroids, comets—and identify Earth's position in it.

Cognitive Complexity: Low to high

Additional Content Areas Addressed

Visual Arts: (VA.5.C.2.1) Revise artwork as a necessary part of the creative process to achieve an artistic goal.

(Continued)

(Continued)

Music: (MU.5.F.2.1) Create a performance, using visual, kinesthetic, digital, and/or acoustic means to manipulate musical elements.

Dance: (DA.5.C.1.3) Demonstrate the use of time, space, effort, and energy to express feelings and ideas through movement. (DA.5.C.2.1) Visualize and experiment with a variety of potential solutions to a given dance problem and explore the effects of each option.

Bloom's Taxonomy

Students move up and down the levels in this activity, depending on their degree of collaboration and the creativity they use to plan, construct, and carry out their assignment.

Multiple Intelligences Included

Logical-Mathematical	Musical/Rhythmic	Naturalist
Spatial	Interpersonal	Bodily/Kinesthetic
Linguistic	Intrapersonal	

ARTS PERCEPTION WORKSHEET

Directions: Read each question completely. Select your choice, and write it on the response line. There are no right or wrong answers, just different. An answer key follows the worksheet.

1. Your students did poorly in the standardized mathematics test. You . . .

    A. Speak to your principal about changing your schedule to add more class time for mathematics and take time away from social studies.
    B. Request a new mathematics textbook.
    C. Look for other creative ways to present the material to the class.

2. In your class, you have several students who are "discipline problems." You . . .

    A. Send the errant students to the principal's office.
    B. Observe those students, and determine what creative instructional strategies might interest them.
    C. Give them "time-out" in the back of the classroom.

3. The following applies to you:
   A. You always wanted to play a musical instrument.
   B. You were not allowed in the chorus when you were in school because you "could not sing."
   C. You took dance class.
   D. You never had an art class but love to draw.
   E. All of these, plus coffee
   F. Some of these

4. You have an artist come into your room six times each semester. You . . .
   A. Are glad to have a free period to catch up on paperwork.
   B. Make sure the students are quiet.
   C. Collaborate with the artist to add measuring and estimating skills into her art project.

5. Arts integration begins with the following:
   A. Written curriculum guides
   B. Workshops given by the administration
   C. Realizing that the arts do enhance all aspects of learning

6. You have an art teacher in your school. You . . .
   A. Have no time in your schedule in order to collaborate.
   B. Have no idea what the art teacher really does in your school except make nice posters for the halls.
   C. Have lunch with the art teacher to learn what he/she does and how you can collaborate.

7. The most important determiner of a student's ability is . . .
   A. An IQ test.
   B. State testing.
   C. An emotional IQ test.
   D. The teacher's observations and assessment of how the student learns and operates in the classroom.
   E. All of these.

8. You have a challenge in keeping the students' attention and getting them to understand a science unit—one that has great focus in the standardized test. You . . .
   A. Take a sabbatical and go on a four-month trip to do "scientific research."

     B. Realize that you may need to change your teaching style and be more creative.

     C. Ask for special testing for the students to determine their problems.

9. The most effective way to support the teaching of a skill is . . .

     A. Implementing computer-assisted activities.

     B. Having the students study the skill for homework using their textbooks.

     C. Creating a hands-on artistic activity that the students can do in a collaborative format.

     D. All of these . . . maybe.

10. Spatial intelligence is the ability to . . .

     A. Think in two dimensions.

     B. Spot a student who is spaced out.

     C. Watch a 3-D film without using the special glasses.

     D. Spot a principal who is spaced out.

     E. None of these.

11. You know that you have musical talent because you . . .

     A. Sing in the shower.

     B. Sing in bars and get applause.

     C. Are able to recognize, create, reproduce, or reflect on music and make choices regarding what music pleases you.

12. Your students just do not yet know the difference between a positive and negative charge. You . . .

     A. Print out another worksheet.

     B. Stick your finger into an open lightbulb socket to demonstrate a positive charge.

     C. Have the students use metal shavings or paper clips on a piece of paper with magnets to demonstrate.

13. In your geometry class, you . . .

     A. Make sure your students color between the lines of the shapes.

     B. Make sure your students understand the purpose of the lines.

     C. Encourage your students to draw the shapes the best they can, and then make choices as to how they want to color them.

14. You never do any singing with your students because you . . .

     A. Have a bad voice.

B. Never get applause when you sing rockabilly in a bar.

C. Can't play the guitar.

D. None of these.

15. You have a unit on measurement coming up in mathematics. You . . .

A. Plan a project that involves the use of rulers, colored pencils, crayons, and paints to introduce the concepts.

B. Teach the concepts from the textbook, and use the activities suggested.

C. Together with your students, plan a project using measuring tools and art supplies that will engage them from start to finish.

16. There is a difference between the "noise of creativity" and the "din of disorder."

A. Yes

B. No

Answer Key

1. C—Analyze the weak areas, and then create lesson plans that actively involve the students in nontraditional and creative ways to address these weaknesses.

2. B—Trust your instincts, and break out of your creative shell. An activity that involves motion or dance might do the trick.

3. E—Grab some coffee or herbal tea, relax, and find your "inner artist." Finish your coffee or tea, and then start creating.

4. C—This answer is way too obvious.

5. C—If you don't agree with this answer, refer to answer #3, replace the coffee or tea with something stronger, please reread Chapters 1 through 3, and make sure to read Chapters 4 through 6.

6. C—Again, way too obvious. Add interest and have lunch off campus. It will do you both a world of good.

7. E—Remember, there is no singular way to assess your students.

8. B—Although answer A might be more alluring, B is the correct answer. However, take a mini-vacation: a few hours alone to change your "mind-set." You might want to review Chapter 2.

9. D—Trust your talent and intuition as a teacher. Also trust your understanding of how each of your students learn; then make decisions on what will work.

10. E—We must, however, note here that B and D are close in the running. Spatial intelligence? Refer back to Chapter 2.

11. C—If you make choices between rock, classical, show tunes, hits of the 1980s, and the many other varieties of music on your radio or device, you have a musical talent. You are making musical choices. Now, how can you apply these musical interests to your teaching?

12. C—If you chose B, this book is of no use to you then, is it?

13. C—Remember, the process is incredibly important in student learning. Perfection does not always need to be present. By the way, if the student's drawn shapes and colors resemble a train wreck, can the student speak about the geometric shapes? There are many ways to assess what a person understands and retains.

14. D—Get over yourself. There are plenty of electronic devices that can assist your singing with your class to add fun to a lesson plan. And for your personal growth, there must be singing classes available somewhere within a 200-mile radius of your home.

15. C—There is nothing better than involving your students in many aspects of the teaching-learning process. And sometimes they come up with an idea that never crossed your mind. Refer again to mind-set in Chapter 2.

16. A—The difference is in how you manage a project and how you interact with your students. The *noise of creativity* should be music to everyone's ears.

WHAT'S COMING?

It is now time for some practical applications. In the next chapter, we look at how teachers can organize their planning to include arts-related activities in the primary grades. Many teachers are already doing this, but there may be some suggestions that you will find both interesting and productive for primary-level students.

Chapter 3—Frequently Asked Questions About Integrating the Arts and STEM

Major Points to Ponder

Jot down key points, ideas, strategies, and resources that you want to consider later.

_____

_____

_____

_____

_____

_____

_____

_____

_____

_____

_____

_____

_____

Chapter 4

Implementing Arts Integration in the Primary Grades (K–4)

The mind of the five-year-old represents, in one sense, the height of creative powers.

—Howard Gardner

Integrating arts-related activities in the primary grades (which, for the purposes of this book, are Grades K–4) is an easy task because the brains of these students are still "free." By free we mean that they are mostly unencumbered by peer pressure to think or act a certain way. They have few or no inhibitions about singing, drawing, or dancing, and they derive great pleasure from these activities. Most still have a growth mind-set, so they believe they can do anything. Their creativity and emotions are nearly unbounded, mainly because the brain's frontal lobe has not developed sufficiently to exert its restraints over uncontrolled creativity and emotions.

Their responses to challenges are quick and reflexive. Abstract thought and divergent thinking are likely present but not well managed.

The brain of this age group is making new connections at an astounding rate as it gathers, interprets, and classifies the signals coming from its environment. These children are already behaving like scientists—trying to understand their world by checking out parts of flowers, turning over rocks, or observing a subway car pull into the station. Occasionally, they even conduct their own crude experiments—with good intentions but not always good outcomes. These explorations help the young brain create patterns that provide meaning about how things work and interact. Neural networks are being built and signal pathways—especially those for acquiring spoken language and learning to read—are being consolidated. With immature frontal lobes, there is little reflective thought, and this age group is willing to let adults make most of the day-to-day decisions for them. Teachers have an opportunity to engage these students in arts-related activities so they can develop cognitive strategies, be creative, socialize with their peers, and experience the gratification and enjoyment of completing an artistic product or performance.

IMPORTANCE OF MOVEMENT

In addition to the rapid growth of cognitive networks, neural pathways that control and coordinate physical motion are also multiplying as the child attempts new challenges, such as swinging a bat, learning to swim, or jumping rope. The development of gross motor skills is crucial during these years because these skills are necessary for survival. They help one jump out of the way of a speeding car or duck fast enough to avoid a punch. For many years, recess time was the official way that nearly all elementary schools acknowledged the importance of taking a break from the classroom and allowing children to engage in play that developed physical as well as social skills. However, recent surveys show that more than 30 percent of the nation's elementary schools have eliminated recess time (Elder & Obel-Omia, 2012), and in those that still have recess, it averages just twenty-seven minutes per day—including time for lunch (Parsad & Lewis, 2006). If this rate continues, regular recess may become just a memory.

Meanwhile, research is revealing how important physical exercise and unstructured play are to maintaining maximum cognitive development. One research study compared four-year-olds enrolled in a preschool that taught traditional phonetics and counting skills to four-year-olds in a preschool that emphasized unstructured play (Diamond, Barnett, Thomas, & Munro, 2007). After one year, those children in the unstructured preschool scored better on a series of crucial cognitive skills that included working memory, attention, and self-control. The researchers suggested that the advantage of unstructured play is that children are most focused when they are having fun. Rather than being frivolous, unstructured play seems to be essential for effective cognitive development.

Recently, the Centers for Disease Control and Prevention (CDC) conducted a review of fifty research studies and found that physical activity during school time helps to improve academic achievement, including grades and standardized test scores (CDC, 2010). They also found no evidence that the time students spent in recess negatively affected their cognitive skills, attitudes, or academic behavior. Neuroscientists tell us that physical activity increases the production of substances that stimulate the creation of new neurons, especially in the hippocampus, the brain's center of learning and memory. With recess on the decline, arts-related activities involving movement become an even more important vehicle for learning in the STEM areas.

SCIENCE, MATHEMATICS, AND THE ARTS IN THE PRIMARY GRADES

Arts-related activities are effective ways of introducing children in this age group to some basic concepts in science and mathematics. Perhaps you have experienced the enjoyment of primary students when they discover the various types of dinosaurs. It is often difficult for them to believe that these creatures are not fantasy monsters but actually roamed our planet millions of years ago. Their study often includes drawing, coloring, and making clay models of different dinosaurs and their habitats. Exploring our solar system also provides numerous opportunities for model-making, singing, and making posters of all types. It is also easy and motivating to use various forms of technology to expand the students' knowledge of these topics.

> *Arts-related activities are effective ways of introducing children in this age group to some basic concepts in science and mathematics.*

Integrating arts-related activities with science, mathematics, and technology with this age group can accomplish three important goals. First, it fosters the students' growth mind-set because they realize they are able to produce different representations of what they are learning in various media. Second, it helps the students to make connections between the arts and science/ mathematics/technology and to view these areas as co-equals rather than as any one being more important than another. Third, as teachers consistently incorporate arts-related activities with STEM topics across these grade levels, the students see no boundaries between and among all these areas. When learners see no boundaries limiting fields of study, creativity and genius often flourish.

Organization of the School and Its Culture

Primary-grade teachers face many curriculum and assessment challenges and juggle numerous managerial demands throughout their day. They also act as "stand-in parents" (remember, *in loco parentis*?) for most waking moments of a child's day. Perhaps more than any other grade level, primary-grade teachers infuse a tremendous amount of nurturing mixed with a strong organizational structure in order to achieve results. It's not an easy task for sure. As we stated earlier, this is a time when children develop cognitive strategies; are creative; learn to socialize; and thrill to the applause of family, friends, and teachers for a job well done. But none of this happens in a vacuum. Before we move into arts integration, let's look at a few issues that have a powerful effect on the instructional environment.

Students of all ages, even adults who attend college later in life, respond to the environment that surrounds them as they learn. This is particularly evident in the primary grades. Elementary schools can vary from grand, century-old brick and stone three-story urban buildings to sprawling, country club-like campuses. Classrooms may be outfitted with the most up-to-date technology or may still rely on the chalkboard. The atmosphere can range from dull and dingy to slick, beautifully bright walls and furniture. Whatever the case, this is the playing field and teachers are the coaches. They must inspire and nudge students along no matter what the surroundings may be. More important than the bricks

> **Without doubt, the culture of a school vastly affects how a teacher can teach and how a student can learn.**

and mortar is the culture of the school. Is it a culture of adventurous learning or staid repetition? Is it a culture that not just welcomes parents and guardians as team members but also provides support so these folks can be of true value in their child's education? Is it a culture that not only accepts other cultures but imbeds such acceptance in all that is taught inside of those walls?

The culture of a school is created by an administration, faculty, and staff who see the potential value in all of the players; who do their best to make the physical plant conducive to a variety of instructional and social learning experiences; and who ensure that students feel safe, cared-for, challenged, and loved. Without doubt, the culture of a school vastly affects how a teacher can teach and how a student can learn.

The Culture Inside The Classroom

You might not be able to control the culture outside of your classroom, but you certainly can do a lot within your four walls. Earlier, we noted that children at this age will allow adults to make the day-to-day decisions for them. Simply put, their minds are like sponges. Make use of this time not only in your active instruction but in your inactive instructional time. In preparing for arts integration, you are not just allowing children to experiment and to take risks but you also are providing surroundings that support such learning.

We have visited primary grade classrooms so overloaded with decorations, posters, and other learning materials that there was not one clear spot in the room. On some occasions, windows were also covered with similar "adornments." It is important to create an environment that is compatible with the cognitive developmental stage of the child's brain. But with so many objects in sight, that brain simply cannot absorb the visual excesses around it. Creativity needs a clean canvas upon which to germinate. Remember the four stages of creative thinking from Chapter 2? There are times when a child needs to incubate ideas by getting relief from the visual distractions in the classroom. When staring at clouds, the child may not be ignoring you but piecing together a few thoughts that you suggested two days earlier. Something just triggered this response, and there was a window and clouds—a perfect combination for incubating a creative thought and bringing it to light. A teacher needs to be sure that the culture of the classroom can support creativity in a structured and manageable way. The culture of the room is the teacher's backdrop, lighting, and set design for the creative performance of teaching.

STEAM STUFF: THE POWER OF VISUALIZATION

 TRY THIS: On one of those days when your students' attention span simply does not seem to exist, stop everything, put the pencils down, close the books, take deep breaths. Coach the kids to look out of the window to relax and dream while looking at the sky. And you do the same. After a few moments, verbally coach them to send "bad stuff" out the window into the sky and to let all of the good learning energies come in to them from the sky. Take a few moments to share what good learning energies came in to them. Then, gently, get back to work. You have spent 3 minutes to save a 30-minute teaching period! That is a good investment of time.

The Culture Outside The Classroom

The learning culture outside of the classroom is created by department chairs, supervisors, building principals, the school board, and parent associations. Many of these individuals may not have a clear understanding of arts integration and how it can further student achievement in the STEM areas. You may be able to turn them into believers by allowing them to see the creative sparks from your students when arts-related activities are integrated with STEM concepts. Of course, if you are fortunate enough to already have supportive leaders, celebrate and raise your own creative bar!

Self-Contained Versus Departmental Organization

Primary grades are typically self-contained with almost all subjects being taught by one teacher. This design hearkens back to earlier times and the one-room schoolhouse when many grades were taught together by one teacher. Although times have changed, this design has not. If you are in a self-contained classroom, you probably have almost complete autonomy in how you teach and in how you organize your classroom. This is a bonus in many ways because you can create the culture for not only arts-integrated instruction but integration of all subjects in a supporting and creative environment. In that way, you get integration of concepts across subject areas with the same lesson plan. (Take a quick look back at Question 5 in Chapter 3.)

Planning Tips for Arts Integration

When creating lesson plans in the self-contained classroom, think of a single, full day as one plan where arts integration takes the lead. In doing so, consider the following:

- Create an active word list that contains new vocabulary for science and social studies with the goals of having the students become comfortable with these words. If you can, have the word list/spelling list mastered *before* the students actually need them. They will feel more confident with the new content because they are familiar with the words, thus making reading and homework a bit more user-friendly.

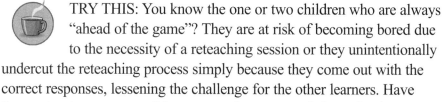

STEAM STUFF: WHEN ART COMES IN HANDY

TRY THIS: You know the one or two children who are always "ahead of the game"? They are at risk of becoming bored due to the necessity of a reteaching session or they unintentionally undercut the reteaching process simply because they come out with the correct responses, lessening the challenge for the other learners. Have them retreat to a corner of the room and create word charts for the upcoming science (or any other) unit. They are challenged and involved and you can get the reteaching done. Win-win at its best!

- Bring together as many content areas as practicable. For example, students learning the difference between a declarative and interrogative sentence in language arts can also create statements about a problem or a question in mathematics or science. Using theater to build out these writing exercises and writing a mystery play involving a mathematics or science unit of study becomes a star-studded arts-integration project!
- If you have music or art teachers in your school, seek their advice. Invite them in to join you in creating the lesson plans and activities and perhaps co-teaching them as well.
- If you have a computer expert in your school, or a computer-savvy parent, ask for their assistance in incorporating the technology into your integrated lesson plans.

Collaboration With Older Students in Mathematics—The "Buddy System" at Its Best!

Sometimes, asking students to teach other students is the best medicine for an aching teaching schedule, not to mention an effective technique for motivation, focus, and retention. Working with a teacher and students in a higher grade can reap great rewards. For instance, we knew of a low-performing elementary school, surrounded by the housing projects in Chicago, where teachers paired up fifth-grade students as buddies to help the second-grade students in mathematics. The teachers coached each grade separately before the first meeting, and then the students were off and running. They met twice weekly for about thirty minutes. These buddies worked together for a year through arithmetic operations and word problems at the second-grade level. The students voted to give up fifteen minutes of their lunchtime, and with some creative scheduling, everyone was happy and productive. Here's what happened:

> *Asking students to teach other students is the best medicine for an aching teaching schedule, not to mention an effective technique for motivation, focus, and retention.*

- Student competence in mathematics operations at *both* grade levels improved dramatically.
- Students in both grades took on ownership of learning and teaching mathematics.
- Frustrated at times, the fifth graders had to become creative in how to teach the second graders, thus allowing the fifth graders to learn new ways to tackle their own challenges in fifth-grade mathematics. Because all students in the school were involved in projects with visiting teaching artists in one way or another, creative solutions began to blossom from the students. With coaching from their teachers, both grades created journals of their work and thoughts about the buddy system. As the projects progressed, grade-level teachers and teaching artists reviewed the students' journals and saw promise and progress in the seemingly random jottings.
- Students in both grade levels showed marked improvement in working with word problems. Although not specifically tested,

teachers observed that the verbal discussions between the students helped both grade levels to understand how to "read a question." Students in the second grade created word problems and various games involving mathematics to challenge their fifth-grade partners and vice versa. Such discussions are almost impossible in a typical classroom with one teacher and thirty students.

- The teachers became coaches. In the beginning, they roamed the classroom, making sure the student interactions were on task and productive. Eventually, they sat to the side and were available for helping to deal with any questions or problems that arose. As both grade levels became fluent with the process, the teachers were an afterthought, much to their chagrin and delight. They learned that they could now raise the bar in other instructional strategies. They also recognized the creative possibilities emerging from the student journals at both grade levels.

- The students really did become "buddies." The second graders wanted to please their newfound pals and do their best. Mathematics became fun!

- Discipline problems disappeared. The students took ownership of the class time, their charges, and their peers, and their creativity flourished. This flowed over into other class activities even when the two grades were not together.

- Another benefit was that this simple process had a remarkable effect on the overall school culture. Because grade levels were crossed, a supportive and caring energy was evident in the cafeteria, auditorium, and hallways. The overriding effect on the entire school culture resulted in a dramatically changed school.

- The students wrote an end-of-year play, based primarily on their journal entries, and presented it to the entire school population. They created lyrics to the melodies of popular tunes. Costumes and sets were colorful, imaginative, and focused on geometric elements. Although the play was not meant to be an instructional tool for the audience, the process of its creation continually fueled interest not only for the students but also for the faculty and staff. Their production, "Math Buddies," was a smash hit!

Arts Integration: A Solo Act or a Duet?

We recognize that the concept of arts integration can be unsettling for some teachers. Primary grade teachers often teach their classes alone. Team teaching is rarely available, so these teachers usually end up working alone on a new project. As a performer, doing a solo act can be gratifying and thrilling. It allows a performer complete autonomy over what and how the act is executed. Yet it is also limiting in that the performance can be myopic in its structure, so a certain part of an audience is not entertained. A duet, however, can enrich each individual's performance, forcing them to delve into otherwise unchartered artistic territory. A form of synergy emerges.

Creating an arts-integrated lesson plan as a solo act, with the teacher acting alone, can be challenging. However, if you review the "Questions" in Chapter 3, you should be able to breathe a bit easier. If you are fortunate to have an arts teacher as the other half of the act, be thankful for this valuable resource. This colleague can offer ideas and perhaps even co-teach with you. Depending on your situation, you may be permitted to bring in a good friend or parent of a student to assist you in an arts-integrated project. This opportunity not only enhances your instructional strategies for the students but enriches your own experience and fuels your STEAM engine. If you have the capability to work with students in another grade level (the buddy system), consider yourself as directing an ensemble, assisting them in blending their talents toward a common learning objective.

For the primary level, we are going to make some suggestions for arts-integrated lesson plans for mathematics and science as a solo act. We offer suggestions for a duet in the following chapter, as these are usually more common in middle school grades. You can adapt either format to your particular situation. Figure 4.2 represents the basic arts-integrated lesson plan with some suggestions. This plan can be copied as a template for your own planning.

IDEAS FOR ARTS-INTEGRATED LESSON PLANS (PRIMARY GRADES)

In Chapter 2, we contrasted a traditional and an arts-integrated approach in an elementary science topic. Here are two more samples of such an approach (also see Figure 4.1).

Grade K—Mathematics

- *Big Idea:* Describe shapes and space
- *Florida Benchmarks:* MA.K.G.2.1–5
- *Cognitive Complexity:* Moderate to high

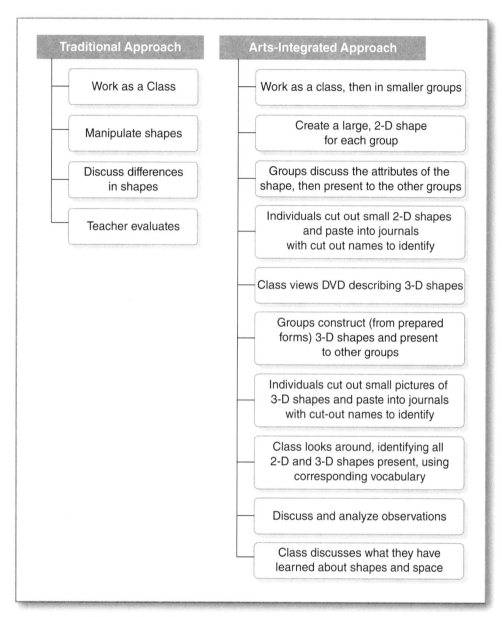

Figure 4.1 Comparison of the traditional and arts-related approaches.

It is important to note that this example (as with all examples in this book) is completely flexible. The intent is to introduce a new strategy, not mandate an exact lesson plan. Remember in Chapter 2 when we refer to changing a mind-set? That is the idea here: to offer an appetizer that will encourage you to create a new STEAM main course (also see Figures 4.2 and 4.3).

Grade 2—Science

- *Big Idea:* Heredity and reproduction: Offspring of plants and animals are similar to, but not exactly like, their parents or each other.
- *Florida Benchmark:* SC.2.L.16.1
- *Cognitive Complexity:* Moderate

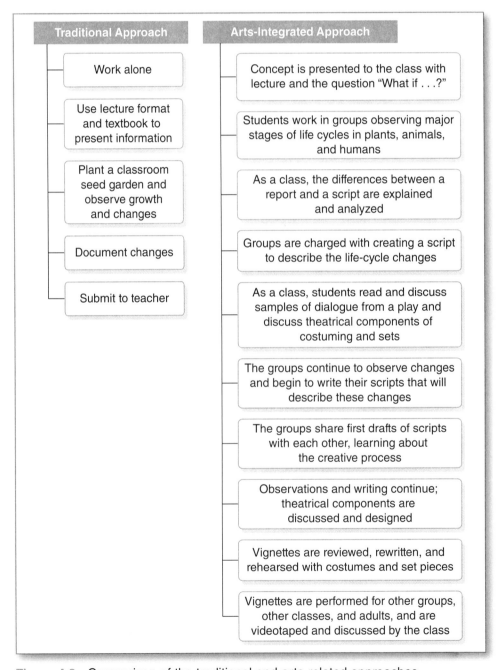

Traditional Approach	Arts-Integrated Approach
Work alone	Concept is presented to the class with lecture and the question "What if . . .?"
Use lecture format and textbook to present information	Students work in groups observing major stages of life cycles in plants, animals, and humans
Plant a classroom seed garden and observe growth and changes	As a class, the differences between a report and a script are explained and analyzed
Document changes	Groups are charged with creating a script to describe the life-cycle changes
Submit to teacher	As a class, students read and discuss samples of dialogue from a play and discuss theatrical components of costuming and sets
	The groups continue to observe changes and begin to write their scripts that will describe these changes
	The groups share first drafts of scripts with each other, learning about the creative process
	Observations and writing continue; theatrical components are discussed and designed
	Vignettes are reviewed, rewritten, and rehearsed with costumes and set pieces
	Vignettes are performed for other groups, other classes, and adults, and are videotaped and discussed by the class

Figure 4.2   Comparison of the traditional and arts-related approaches.

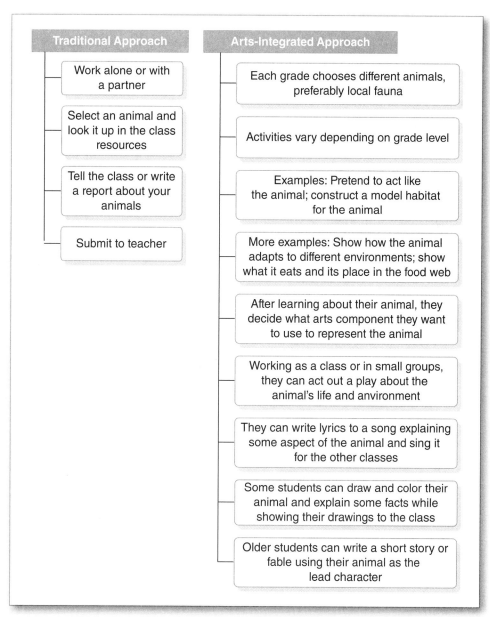

Figure 4.3   Comparison of the traditional and arts-related approaches.

Multigrade Arts-Related Activities About Different Animals

This STEAM lesson plan might seem unwieldy at first glance, but with planning and adaptation to your classes' abilities, it can work. This is a good example of an arts-integrated lesson plan that can cover the course of a few weeks or even months. Unfortunately, the bean seed and the butterfly larvae follow their own lesson plans, so be aware of your timing. This plan can be interspersed with other science topics, thus alleviating any wasted time. Our experience is that the students will be so excited that they will make sure that the project moves along. Having help from a friend who is an artist or who teaches art or theater is invaluable in this exercise.

This example outline for an arts-integrated lesson plan is a good way to get started. Again, it might seem like a burden at first, but after working through it, you will see that many of the components are things you already have done before. This will give you the confidence to move into new, uncharted arts-integration territory. Here is a lesson plan format designed for one teacher. It contains suggestions to guide you through the planning process. Feel free to use it as a template for your STEAM lessons, and remember to have fun. You will find more ideas for STEAM lessons at various grade levels in Chapters 7 and 8.

Sample Primary Grade Arts-Integration Lesson Plan Format

One Teacher

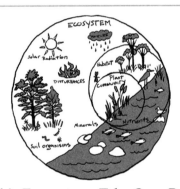

Title of Project: Earth's Ecosystems Take Over Room 5

Primary Curriculum Subject: Science
   Benchmarks: SC.5.E.7.1–6

Integrated Curriculum Subjects: Reading and language arts
   Benchmarks: LA.5.1.6.3–5, LA.5.1.6.9

Primary Art Form: Visual art
   Benchmarks: VA.5.C.1.1, VA.5.C.2.4, VA.5.C.3.1–2

Integrated Art Form: Music
   Benchmarks: MU.5.H.1.1, MU.5.H.1.3

Benchmarks are from the State of Florida but are very similar to those in other states.

Management Planning

Schedule

- **Number of Sessions:** 10
- **Length of Sessions:** Varies depending on lesson plan
- **Specific Dates/Times:** N/A

Materials Needed: Large rolls of kraft paper, found objects, tempera, markers, clay, scissors, tape, zip ties, other materials depending on the creativity of the students, notebooks (see note in the assessment section), very simple audio equipment.

If project is to take place in a space other than your classroom:

- **Other spaces to be used:** N/A
- **Appropriate planning with school staff:** N/A

Notes: Predetermine how these installations can be done safely and sensibly in your classroom, keeping in mind typical day-to-day activity that takes place in the room.

MULTIPLE INTELLIGENCES APPLICATIONS

Check all that will be included in the project.

- _X_ Linguistic
- ___ Logical/Mathematical
- _X_ Musical
- ___ Bodily/Kinesthetic
- _X_ Visual/Spatial
- _X_ Naturalist
- _X_ Interpersonal
- _X_ Intrapersonal

BLOOM'S TAXONOMY APPLICATIONS

Check all that will be included in the project.

- _X_ Create
- _X_ Evaluate
- _X_ Analyze
- _X_ Apply
- _X_ Understand
- _X_ Remember

Assessment Methods: Portfolio, journals, written quizzes, and tests as mandated locally. At the culmination of the project, the classroom should be open for visitation by other classes and guests.

The notebooks are an ongoing source of formative assessment for both the teacher and student. Depending on your situation, this may be a traditional paper notebook involving handwriting and cutting and pasting of samples or an electronic format. Whatever the case, this is a vital part of the ongoing project and it involves creative thinking that we discussed in Chapter 2.

Session One

Date/Time: N/A

Aim of the Lesson: (1) To introduce how humans continue to explore interactions among water, air, and land. (2) To introduce the project: creating various Earth ecosystems throughout the entire classroom using art materials and recorded music.

The Plan: Students will watch a video describing various Earth ecosystems and will begin to create a notebook/journal containing all of their research and notes. Appropriate use of the textbook can also be useful. Students will discuss all of the options for changing their classroom into a myriad of Earth ecosystems, focusing on the creative possibilities while recognizing the limitations brought about by safety requirements. This is a big but enjoyable project.

Session Two

Date/Time: N/A

Aim of the Lesson: (1) To review the information presented in Session One. (2) To direct how collaboration in small groups will take place. (3) To determine the projects for each group.

(Continued)

(Continued)

The Plan: In an open discussion format, students discuss what they remember from the previous lesson. They will be coached to define differences in air (movement of air, storms, etc.), water (oceans, rain, etc.), and land (forests, deserts, urban centers, etc.). After these broad descriptions, students are divided into groups, each tasked with creating a "larger than life" artistic representation of desert, rain forest, ocean, mountain range, urban center, etc. After grouping the students, all groups will be directed to brainstorm what their particular area looks like and to list its particular characteristics. All groups will share the results of their discussions with the entire class. By sharing creative ideas, other ideas should emerge from the ensuing groups. You may want to employ a bit of social studies and have each group elect a spokesperson if time permits.

Sanity Check: By this point, you will have a good idea of the breadth of the projects your students will be creating. You want to think carefully about placement of the projects in your room to assure that no catastrophes happen during their creation. Having this information will help you to coach your students as they let their creative spirits go wild. For example, a ten-foot papier-mâché mountain might be a bit too much. Determine where each group will ultimately install their completed project. The final installations will literally surround the classroom and perhaps even flow outside the classroom door.

Session Three

Date/Time: N/A

Aim of the Lesson: (1) To introduce vocabulary: water cycle, evaporation, precipitation (rain, snow, sleet, and hail), temperature, barometric pressure, humidity, wind speed, environment, latitude, and elevation (additional words as needed). (2) To review the overall plan and organizational and housekeeping directives.

The Plan: Using your skills as a reading teacher, the vocabulary is presented in a way that works for you and your class. The vocabulary list and definitions, usage samples, etc., are an active part of the notebook/journal. Journal entries are shared verbally.

Sessions Four, Five, Six, Seven, and Eight

Date/Time: N/A

Aim of the Lesson: Students continue to research their particular area and with coaching cover all necessary information. The stages of the creative process are reviewed so that students understand that it may take a number of trials and errors before the final product is created. After discussion and preliminary sketches in their notebooks, the groups present the concept for their project to the entire class along with the list of supplies they will need. This discussion should be exciting and have no surprises, assuming coaching has been taking place. After you approve the plans, the students can begin their projects.

The Plan: Each session begins with you asking, "How are we doing?" Encourage discussion and sharing of ideas. Students work in their groups, using their research to guide the creation of their projects. As the projects take shape, installations can begin.

For Example: The group working with the ocean may decide to create an underwater area. Walls may need to be covered with blue art paper or fabric and part of the floor with sandy colored paper or fabric. Rocks and coral can be created out of altered and painted cardboard boxes and clay. Ocean life can be created from art paper and found objects (buttons for fish eyes) and can be suspended from the ceiling using string.

Sanity Check: If you have the flexibility, it might be better to take an entire afternoon to get a good two hours of continual work done rather than using the regularly scheduled class time. Remember, set-up and cleanup times are harsh realities. You might get more accomplished in creating larger blocks of working time and changing your schedule a bit.

Sessions Nine and Ten

Date/Time: N/A

Aim of the Lesson: To review all content information and begin the completion of all projects.

The Plan: Coach the students in the completion of their projects. This is where the student frustration might appear, and this could become the proverbial "teachable moment." Coaching a disappointed student who is having to make a choice because of lack of time or because something just did not work out is problem solving at its best. Remember, there is often no single solution, and students should learn that there are multiple ways to make their point. For instance, what if the ten pounds of cotton balls just won't stay glued together and the cumulus clouds are just not happening? Then consider white pillowcases stuffed with a few balloons, tied or pinned (very carefully), closed and suspended from the ceiling using zip ties or hangers.

Music and Sound Effects: This can be challenging, but remember that there is a difference between the noise of creativity and the din of disorder. Rainforest sounds, ocean waves, and bird and animal sounds can all be used in the same room but with specific directives as to the size and kind of audio equipment and the volume level. We suggest that the students choose the music and sounds, but the volume level is the teacher's decision.

Sanity Check: Some groups may be finished while others are still hard at work. To avoid boredom and possible behavior challenges, assign these groups the task of drawing invitations that will be delivered to the principal, school staff, and other classes to attend this massive work of science and art.

Session Eleven and More

Date/Time: N/A

Aim of the Lesson: To have the students display and explain their projects. Each group is the expert in its area and shares its knowledge with the other groups. The projects are shared with other classes, school administration, staff, and parents.

The Plan: Students verbally explain their project and what it represents. Other groups and guests walk through, touch, and otherwise experience the project.

An Idea: A project of this scope deserves publicity. Get the word out, and maybe the local paper or news station will come by and do a piece. This is a great way to publicize the great work of the students, the teacher, and the school.

Sample Primary Grade Arts-Integration Lesson Plan Format

One Teacher

Title of Project: _____

Primary Curriculum Subject: _____

    Benchmarks: _____

    _____

Integrated Curriculum Subjects: _____

    Benchmarks: _____

    _____

Primary Art Form: _____

    Benchmarks: _____

    _____

Integrated Art Forms: _____

    Benchmarks: _____

    _____

STEAM STUFF

In reality, you could address literally hundreds of benchmarks in one project. Stay focused on only the benchmarks that you will actually assess during and at the end of the project.

Management Planning

Schedule

- Number of sessions: _____
- Length of sessions: _____
- Specific dates/times: _____

Materials needed: _____
_____

If project is to take place in a space other than your classroom:

- Other spaces to be used:
- Appropriate planning with school staff:

Notes:

STEAM STUFF
Be very specific in your time and scheduling needs from the start. A good plan can always be modified to accommodate unforeseen circumstances.

MULTIPLE INTELLIGENCES APPLICATIONS

Check all that will be included in the project.

___ Linguistic

___ Logical/Mathematical

___ Musical

___ Bodily/Kinesthetic

___ Visual/Spatial

___ Naturalist

___ Interpersonal

___ Intrapersonal

STEAM STUFF
You want to include each intelligence at least once during your project to be sure you are addressing the many learning styles of your students.

← Use this as a "sanity check" to be sure you are including various applications. Remember, your students may move among levels during a project.

→

BLOOM'S TAXONOMY APPLICATIONS

Check all that will be included in the project.

___ Create

___ Evaluate

___ Analyze

___ Apply

___ Understand

___ Remember

Complexity ↑

Assessment methods:

STEAM STUFF

Be sure to incorporate many formative assessments, as well as adhering to your local requirements.

Session One

Date/Time:

Aim of the Lesson:

The Plan:

STEAM STUFF

The number of sessions will depend on many factors. Be sure to give yourself plenty of instructional time—maybe even some extra time if possible, just in case!

Session Two

Date/Time:

Aim of the Lesson:

The Plan:

Session Three

Date/Time:

Aim of the Lesson:

The Plan:

Session Four

Date/Time:

Aim of the Lesson:

The Plan:

Session Five

Date/Time:

Aim of the Lesson:

The Plan:

Session Six

Date/Time:

Aim of the Lesson:

The Plan:

WHAT'S COMING?

Experienced teachers know that middle school can be quite a challenge for students as they move from familiar, self-contained classrooms to a less personal, departmentalized structure. Arts-integrated lessons may make that transition into the STEM subject-centered classes easier because these types of lessons can be motivating and stress-reducing. In the next chapter, we offer suggestions for integrating arts-related activities into STEM courses. All of these suggestions have been successful in other middle schools.

Chapter 4—Implementing Arts Integration in the Primary Grades (K–4)

Major Points to Ponder

Jot down key points, ideas, strategies, and resources that you want to consider later.

_____

_____

_____

_____

_____

_____

_____

_____

_____

_____

_____

_____

_____

_____

Chapter 5

Implementing Arts Integration in the Intermediate Grades (5–8)

The mass media heap out unrelenting doses of prefabricated images to children.... As a result, kids simply sit back and passively drink in these images, which then proceed to seep into the subconscious only to emerge in school as stereotypical drawings, stories filled with clichés, and artificial and unreal conceptions of how the world works.

—Thomas Armstrong

During these preadolescent years, brain growth and development continue at a remarkable pace. Growth and development may seem the same, but biologist Robert Sylwester (2010) makes a clear distinction between them. He suggests that growth implies an increase in some existing condition, such as in size or in a particular competency. We *nurture* growth. Development, on the other hand, describes the modification or addition of structures or abilities. We *observe* development. Fertilizing a plant nurtures its growth, and we can see it develop new branches, leaves, and roots. As students grow in their ability to do addition, they develop their multiplication skills.

You will recall from Chapter 2 that by the age of ten to twelve years, the emotional brain is fully developed. The rational brain is still maturing and will do so until the age of twenty-two to twenty-four years. But it *is* developing and therefore beginning to exert more influence over the middle-school students' thought processes and reactions. Students' responses to challenges are now delayed, less impulsive, and more reflective. The frontal lobes are more actively involved in decision making and are capable of dealing with more abstract concepts and challenges involving divergent thinking. Meanwhile, the social brain is also maturing, and these students begin to measure the social impact of their behavior on their peers. Cultural differences become more evident, as do cultural biases and prejudices—all of which may have an impact on the classroom's emotional climate.

> *The emotional bond between teacher and student [in middle schools] is much weaker than in the self-contained classrooms [of the earlier grades].*

Recall that this is the grade span where surveys show that only 50 percent of the students believe they are creative, down from 95 percent in the earlier grades (Lehrer, 2012a). Why is that? The students' carefree days of the earlier grades are gone. Now, most of their STEM teachers are content specialists who may see each student for as little as forty-five minutes a day. Consequently, the emotional bond between teacher and student is much weaker than in the self-contained classrooms. Teacher instructional presentations are more predictable and the STEM curriculum more content-heavy than ever. Teachers feel the need to "cover the material," so differentiated instruction is minimal. Assessment is mostly paper-and-pencil tests involving convergent thinking. Novelty is rare; conformity is the expectation. The impact of movement on learning that we discussed in Chapter 4 is greater for this age group because they are aware of more elements in their environment that can distract them from the learning objective. Although their attention span is not less, the *demands* for their attention increase. Movement helps greatly with focus.

Integrating arts-related activities with STEM becomes more essential now as they can help provide the novelty that otherwise diminishes rapidly in these grades. For example, performance assessments can replace some of the written tests by giving students the option to demonstrate what they have learned through making music, drawing, or doing some other art form. Project-based learning modules are an excellent means of understanding science concepts because they often involve a mix of STEM areas while simultaneously achieving the common-core science standard of crosscutting concepts.

A DAY IN THE LIFE OF A
MIDDLE SCHOOL STUDENT

The journey from Grade 3 to Grade 5 is a social awakening that often becomes the center of interest for these developing students. As a result, a teacher can feel more like a social director on a cruise line than an educator. Middle school students not only have their blossoming social lives generating daily drama but they are also surrounded by social media that heighten their ability to respond to many situations in a not-so-responsible fashion. Keep this very real social situation in mind as we address learning preferences and instructional strategies and search for creative ways to make use of these environmental influences.

Basically, the use of computers, cell phones, and other devices *is* technology education. We rarely teach it in school because the students learn on their own and from each other. When was the last time typing/ keyboarding was taught in school? Since students live with computers, should we not be teaching proper typing skills in middle school to increase

> *If today's teachers are going to relate . . . with their students, they need to know what is providing them fun and entertainment.*

efficiency? In middle school, technology is understood and taken for granted, so we must make the best use of it. Including appropriate and creative technology programs in your lesson plans can be immensely effective and engaging for your students. You might not be able to solve all of their social woes, but you can certainly learn what games they are playing and what social media they are using. Back in the day (depending on how far back you go), it was a sock hop or a disco that helped middle school students have fun and experience an appropriate social environment. If today's teachers are going to relate on any level with their students, they need to know what is providing them fun and entertainment. But then, you knew that already!

Departmental Organization

Middle schools are becoming more departmentalized, both instructionally and even in the actual design of the school itself. In such structures, the teachers tend to be content specialists, and due to the ever-increasing demands on teachers for improved test scores, they rarely venture outside the boundaries of their curriculum area. This is where we see the unraveling of the "liberal arts" way of thinking. In order for arts integration to succeed, departmental teachers need to move past their structural and mental barriers and the traditions of their own schooling. Educational reformer Deborah Meier states the following:

> Change cannot be undertaken by a faculty that is not convinced and involved. Even when teachers are engaged, it's tough to change the habits of a lifetime, embedded as such habits are in the way we talk about schooling and the way our students and their families expect it to be delivered. (Meier, 1995, p. 107)

This, of course, is easier said than done, and therein lies the rub. The STEM initiative is not just about adding more STEM courses but about getting teachers to recognize how each of the areas of STEM interact and to reach out to other teachers—including non-STEM teachers—to improve students' critical thinking skills and creativity. Departmentalization may make sense for management reasons, but it can be a constraint to collaboration. At its best, collaboration and integration can bring good teachers to the realization that they can be even better at what they do.

To be fair, departmental teachers also have the real issue of brick and mortar walls, offices, and concourses that almost by their nature impede collaboration, reinforcing the "stay in your own area" thinking. What we are talking about here is the rigidity of instruction that the high stakes of standardized testing demands. Our task is to find ways to work with and around the constraints of standardized testing so that both teacher and students have those rewarding "aha" moments. One of the authors, when principal of an elementary school, made the case for not increasing the reading periods by five minutes by noting that the students were actually learning reading in their four periods of chorus every week. Many of the lyrics the students sang were new words to them, expanding their vocabulary, and seeing these new words in context provided meaning. It was an uphill battle, but in the end, reading scores rose significantly. At that time, there was no research to back up that choice as there is now. Know your goals, let go of a mind-set or two, look forward, and be creative! And have fun!

Challenges of Middle School Schedules

One of the greatest challenges to incorporating successful arts integration projects is the day-to-day schedule of a middle school. Teachers rarely have control over their schedule, but they can control what happens when they close the classroom door. In addition to the crowded regular schedule, there is always something special or unexpected that crops up that can change a two-week project into a four-week marathon. Do not despair. The fact that you know what we mean by this already indicates that you are a good planner for emergencies. The most important thing to remember about creating arts-integrated projects with STEM is that they must be the antithesis of the daily stress and grind for the students and for you as well. Allow flexibility so that the creativity that you will have invested in the project—either alone or with another teacher or teaching artist—will not

> *Arts-integrated projects with STEM . . . must be the antithesis of the daily stress and grind for the students and for [the teacher] as well.*

be dashed to the rocks when unexpected events occur. You will be able to not only engage your students, but inspire them to be creative.

Keeping Students Interested: Comparing Music and Science

Let's look at one of the Grade 6 science standards titled, "The Characteristics of Scientific Knowledge" with the benchmark, "Distinguishing science from other activities involving thought" (FL: SC.6.N.2.1). In Grade 6? This seems like a difficult assignment, and you cannot run away from the fact that this, along with other benchmarks, eventually will be assessed in a standardized test. Given this challenge, here is one way to approach it with arts integration:

Think of the major points you want students to learn: Scientific knowledge is ever changing and evolving. We now know that there are innumerable solar systems beyond our own, a relatively new revelation in the past fifty years. Scientists are continually making new discoveries, using the scientific method as their framework. Good to know, but how can you interest middle school brains in this notion that scientific pursuits are different from those in other areas of human endeavor?

Now think for a moment about the music of your teen years, and listen to the music your current students love. Consider a contest where students vote to pick the best song of the week. (This will involve a bit of social studies and the democratic process.) Have them listen and write down the differences between one of your favorite songs and one of theirs. What has changed in the music? How is music produced today different from thirty years ago? Because of their vast media exposure, the students can have a high-level discussion by comparing and contrasting their findings.

What has happened here? They are engaged, and they are hooked because *they* chose one of the songs. However, the original objective was *distinguishing science from other activities involving thought.* Now ask them how their discussion about music is different from how scientists would talk about the results of their experiments. They may find that, unlike music, scientific thought has these characteristics:

- Is based on empirical evidence and appropriate for understanding the natural world
- Provides only a limited understanding of the supernatural, aesthetic or other ways of knowing, such as religion and philosophy
- Is open to change
- Strives for objectivity (However, because science is practiced by humans, there is always the risk that some subjective notions may creep in.)

Students were engaged in higher-order thinking (comparing and contrasting), which is Bloom's analysis level. During their discussion, and with guidance from you, they focused on the nature of scientific thought as compared to thought about how music has changed over the years. Objective accomplished, and all for a song!

Better yet, this is not a one-time deal. Because of its relevancy and high interest level, this strategy using music can be imbedded in other curriculum areas, and even discussed outside the classroom as part of homework assignments. By doing so, you help students see how discussions about the arts can lead to understanding about the nature of inquiry in the STEM areas. With time, arts-related activities can become part of the dialogue in every STEM-to-STEAM class.

TEACHER TO TEACHER COLLABORATIONS

Take a colleague to dinner. Get away from the classroom and the faculty room. Collaboration is one of those things, much like surfing, that in order to do it, you just need to do it! In the truest sense, collaboration is when teachers get together and bring their strengths and weaknesses to the table. Because we are focusing on arts integration, take a quick look back at Chapter 3 and review what we list as "The Arts." In getting to know your fellow teachers on a personal level, you might discover a hidden painter, a latent gardener, a professional singer, a slightly out-of-shape dancer whose "inner artist" just needs to be supported and nurtured. Through authentic discussion and activity, teachers encourage and enrich each other to bring newfound gifts to their instruction and to their students. Such teamwork is invaluable and can be downright fun! And this fun will wash over and enrich what you collectively do for the students. There is no better way to model working together for young minds than to actually do it. Students watching two adults work in harmony does a lot for their personal growth, and it offers a model that they can use when they have to collaborate on STEAM projects.

STEM Teacher and Arts Teacher Collaborations

Our experience is that you can raise the STEM-to-STEAM bar if you have the good fortune to have art and/or music teachers in your school. It is even better if they are friendly and not completely overworked without a moment to spare. Typically, this is the case, so you want to be considerate of their time and go to them with specifics. Most probably, they will not have time to brainstorm. They need to know right away how they can help you and, if possible, work with you. Have your material researched with enough background information in your hand when you meet. Go to them after having gone through your own artistic process and suitable time has been spent on the preparation and incubation of your project. Be as specific as possible. Remember, you are not telling them what art you want; you are *asking* them how they as an artist can help you create an amazing STEAM lesson plan or unit. Meet them with your questions ready.

Some teachers of the arts may not have had experience with real collaboration in a classroom. We must state here that we are talking many levels above the request of a music teacher to "Please come in and teach a song about Pluto"! Now, you may still be lamenting Pluto's demise as a "real planet," but that cannot be your driving force. Most music teachers can bring a lot more to your STEAM lesson plan. Asking art teachers, for example, if they have an idea how the students can create a solar system in your classroom that has actual relative sizes of the planets, their moons, and the sun is a much deeper activity. You provide the scientific data, the art teacher provides the artistic activities, and a lesson plan is born. If, unfortunately, you do not have an art or music teacher, or you do but they are not cooperative, resort to the previous section or the next section.

STEM Teacher and Guest Teaching Artist Collaborations

Teaching artists are the holy grail of arts integration in schools at every level. We noted in Chapter 2 that excellent teaching artists are trained, and they can speak your language—pedagogy. They understand your needs, know about state standards, and have probably overcome many obstacles in their careers in schools. Experienced teaching artists will bring a lot of information and ideas, while newer teaching artists will bring their artistic ability and training but will rely more on your educational and classroom wisdom for guidance. Whatever the case, you are the lead teacher so, as stated in the previous section, you need to know what you want. The lesson plan formats in this chapter will give you an idea of how to approach this collaborative process. Remember, you are not changing your *goals* for the lesson plan but changing your *approach* to the lesson plan. At the end of the collaboration, both you and the students should be reveling in a successful, creative, and fun experience. There are a number of resources for locating teaching artists, and they can usually be found through your local arts council or community arts center. Refer to the Resources for additional suggestions.

Let's Hit the Road! Making a STEAM Class Trip Relevant

Students love a trip out of the classroom. The great thing about a class trip is that the students are so excited you can sneak the learning in and they are none the wiser. With so many restrictions on trips due to schedules, testing, tight budgets, and concerns for safety, many districts now mandate outcomes-based class trips. Administrators want to be assured that the trip is an integral part of a required learning objective. Take advantage of class trips for STEAM lessons with these suggestions in mind:

- Plan so that the trip and the experience are an integral part of your instructional strategy, not an afterthought.
- You want the students to enjoy the experience, so keep forms and paperwork to a minimum. Be sure that you have done the pre-trip preparation in the classroom well beforehand so that the activities on the trip have meaning and purpose. Think about using journals and a pencil to draw things that they see and take simple notes. Cameras are an amazing tool—especially if you have printing capabilities in your school. Depending on your situation, this is when you want the students to be able to use their cell phone cameras.
- Choose a trip where teaching will be done by the venue staff. Your job is to coach on a trip, not to teach. Be sure that your guide knows as soon as practicable exactly what points you want to have made. Good guides and docents will welcome your interest in what they have to say and will work with you and the students.
- Review your school district's policy for trips, and be sure that you have enough assistance with the students to achieve your outcomes. You might want one or two additional chaperones.
- Have a specific wrap-up lesson planned for when you return from the trip. A presentation by the students to another class is always a good way to share the experience.

Guidelines for the Lesson Plan Format

This lesson plan format may seem burdensome, but keep in mind that it is designed for an extended arts-integration project that may be part of a larger unit of study. For example, you might be spending a few weeks on working with 2-D and 3-D figures, analyzing them using distance and angles. Knowing the temperament, capabilities, and needs of your students, you opt to create an arts-integrated lesson plan for three sessions focusing on the validation of the Pythagorean Theorem by finding distances in real world situations.

"Big Idea" and Objective

In this case, the "Big Idea" might be the analysis of 2-D and 3-D figures and the specific objective would be "validation of the Pythagorean Theorem."

Benchmarks

If someone sat in the back of your classroom and noted every curriculum benchmark you covered—directly or indirectly—in your specific content area as well as all others, the number would be enormous. In planning, list only the benchmarks you will assess. In this case, less is actually more.

Three Essential Questions

An essential question is the essence of what you believe students should learn in the short time they are with you. The questions can begin on a lower level of Bloom's Taxonomy with the goal of ending on a higher level. For example, a second grade unit on weather could have the following three questions:

> **An essential question is . . . what you believe students should [know, understand, or be able to do] in the short time they are with you.**

1. What is weather? (Remember level)

2. What kinds of weather do we experience where we live? (Understand level)

3. How are tornadoes and hurricanes the same? How are they different? (Analysis level)

And a fifth-grade series of essential questions on a similar unit might look like this:

1. What are the different kinds of weather? (Remember level)

2. Explain in your own words how meteorologists study weather? (Understand level)

3. What information would you need to know to predict tomorrow's weather? Get it and make a prediction. (Application level)

Of course, there is nothing magic about the number three. You might ask four or five questions. We suggest that the minimum number should be three most of the time to ensure that the students' mental processing is moving from convergent to divergent thinking. In the end, the single most important question facing you as the teacher is "What do I want my students to know, understand, and be able to do when we have completed the lesson(s)?"

Management Planning

These issues can make or break a great plan. Forgetting to collaborate with the school maintenance staff might be disastrous, finding there is no available water hookup after you and your students planned and planted a vegetable garden. A prepared list sent to parents, local businesses, etc., in advance of the project can be helpful for you and your students.

Multiple Intelligences and Bloom's Taxonomy Applications

Howard Gardner's *Multiple Intelligences Theories* and the revised *Bloom's Taxonomy* are useful guides when planning an arts integration project. Familiarize yourself with both concepts (see Chapter 9).

New Vocabulary

As an educator, you know that student achievement in mathematics and science can depend largely on reading skills, especially vocabulary. Before you begin a new unit of study, gradually introduce any new vocabulary. Clever teachers recognize that visual exposure does help retention of learning. Have a list of ten new vocabulary words artistically displayed in the front of the classroom a week or two before you begin a unit, say on properties of matter (Grade 8). The list will intrigue students and may generate questions and novelty. Create some fun by having a small contest the day you begin the unit, seeing who has figured out the definitions of *density, thermal conductivity, solubility,* and *magnetic properties.* The very nature of the game has the students actively engaged in *using* the vocabulary, and they are steps ahead in comprehending the material.

Assessment Methods

Be sure to vary your assessments as much as you can while keeping within the guidelines of your school's policies. Asking students to write in a journal incorporates all forms of literacy and aids in comprehension. Formative assessment is the most productive method of knowing what your students know, understand, and can do. Simply put, the function of formative assessment is to help teachers and students decide when and how they need to make adjustments to what they are doing in order to achieve the learning objective(s) (Popham, 2008). Incorporate what will work for you in your situation, but be sure to include creative methods, such as performance and portfolio assessments as well.

Grade 7—Science

- *Big Idea—Title of Project:* Energy Transfer and Transformations
- *Florida Benchmarks:* SC.7.P.11.1–4
- *Cognitive Complexity:* Moderate—High (See Figure 5.1.)

Grade 6—Mathematics

This project was done in a sixth-grade classroom of twenty-three students with a teacher and a teaching artist. Their planning consisted of three, one-hour sessions. The project took more time than anticipated due to the enthusiasm and unleashed creativity of the students. It took ten, one-hour classes that were team taught over the course of six weeks. Students gladly worked on the project during lunch periods and at home. On "Carnival Day," students from the other fourth and fifth grades came into the classroom to play the games.

Language arts and reading played a big part in this project when it came to describing and creating the directions for the games. The resulting project not only met the benchmarks but also included understanding the nature of probability, the solar system, water and air pressure, and board games that involved mathematical processes.

- *Big Idea—Title of Project:* Understanding of and fluency with multiplication and division of fractions and decimals; write, interpret and use mathematical expressions and equations.

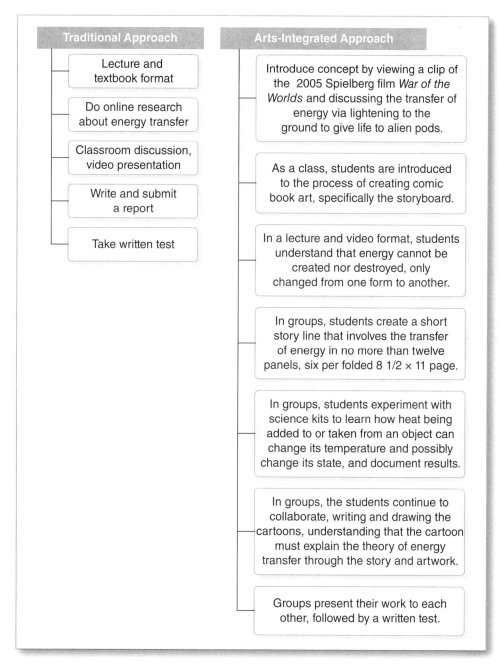

Traditional Approach

- Lecture and textbook format
- Do online research about energy transfer
- Classroom discussion, video presentation
- Write and submit a report
- Take written test

Arts-Integrated Approach

- Introduce concept by viewing a clip of the 2005 Spielberg film *War of the Worlds* and discussing the transfer of energy via lightening to the ground to give life to alien pods.
- As a class, students are introduced to the process of creating comic book art, specifically the storyboard.
- In a lecture and video format, students understand that energy cannot be created nor destroyed, only changed from one form to another.
- In groups, students create a short story line that involves the transfer of energy in no more than twelve panels, six per folded 8 1/2 × 11 page.
- In groups, students experiment with science kits to learn how heat being added to or taken from an object can change its temperature and possibly change its state, and document results.
- In groups, the students continue to collaborate, writing and drawing the cartoons, understanding that the cartoon must explain the theory of energy transfer through the story and artwork.
- Groups present their work to each other, followed by a written test.

Figure 5.1   Comparison of the traditional and arts-related approaches.

- *Florida Benchmarks:* MA.6.A.1.1–3, MA.6.A.3.1, 3–6 (and many more)
- *Cognitive Complexity:* Low—Moderate—High

Figure 5.2 shows a fully completed arts-integration plan for multiple lessons on measuring geometric shapes that can be adapted to several elementary grade levels.

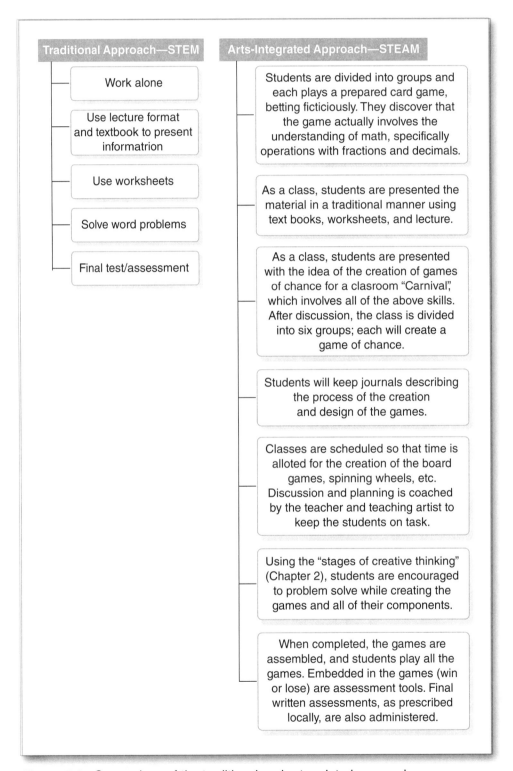

Traditional Approach—STEM	Arts-Integrated Approach—STEAM
Work alone	Students are divided into groups and each plays a prepared card game, betting ficticiously. They discover that the game actually involves the understanding of math, specifically operations with fractions and decimals.
Use lecture format and textbook to present informatrion	As a class, students are presented the material in a traditional manner using text books, worksheets, and lecture.
Use worksheets	As a class, students are presented with the idea of the creation of games of chance for a clasroom "Carnival", which involves all of the above skills. After discussion, the class is divided into six groups; each will create a game of chance.
Solve word problems	Students will keep journals describing the process of the creation and design of the games.
Final test/assessment	Classes are scheduled so that time is alloted for the creation of the board games, spinning wheels, etc. Discussion and planning is coached by the teacher and teaching artist to keep the students on task.
	Using the "stages of creative thinking" (Chapter 2), students are encouraged to problem solve while creating the games and all of their components.
	When completed, the games are assembled, and students play all the games. Embedded in the games (win or lose) are assessment tools. Final written assessments, as prescribed locally, are also administered.

Figure 5.2 Comparison of the traditional and arts-related approaches.

Sample Intermediate Grades
Arts-Integration Lesson Plan Format

Teacher With Collaborating Teaching Artist
Teacher and Teaching Artists = Collaborative Lessons
Teacher Alone = Activities Between Sessions

The "Big Idea"—Main Topic or Theme: "Measuring Madness"

Objective of the Arts-Integrated Project: Students will learn the following:

- About 3-D geometric shapes and their measurement
- Measurement techniques and vocabulary
- Organizational skills and information management
- To work collaboratively through problem solving and contrasting/comparing their work against set standards and benchmarks

Plan Created By: Ms. X

Assisted By: Ms. Y

Primary Curriculum Subject: Math

    Benchmarks: MA.4.G.5.3-MA.5.G.3.1-2

Integrated Curriculum Subjects: Language Arts, Technology

    Benchmarks: SL.5.1, 2, 4; L.5.1, 2, 4; W.5.2, 4, 7

Primary Art Form: Visual Art

    Benchmarks: VA.5.F.1.1, 2; VA.5.F.2.3, VA.5.F.3.3, VA.5.C.1.2

Integrated Arts Forms: None

    Benchmarks: (Not applicable)

Planning Responsibilities
List the responsibilities of
each teacher and/or teaching artist with
"due dates" to keep everyone on track.

NAME:

RESPONSIBILITY(IES) AND DUE DATES:

NAME:

RESPONSIBILITY(IES) AND DUE DATES:

NAME:

RESPONSIBILITY(IES) AND DUE DATES:

NAME:

RESPONSIBILITY(IES) AND DUE DATES:

Three Essential Questions (Comprehension):

EQ 1: What are geometric shapes?
    Bloom's Application: Understand

EQ 2: How do we measure geometric shapes?
    Bloom's Application: Analysis

EQ 3: How are geometric shapes used in our day-to-day lives and why?
    Bloom's Application: Evaluation

Management Planning

Schedule

- **Number of Sessions:** 10
- **Length of Sessions:** 30 minutes to 1 hour
- **Specific Dates/Times:** TBD

Materials Needed: Empty notebooks, rulers, pencils, crayons, markers, chart paper for brainstorming (for each student), white board, printed patterns, glue sticks, clear tape, scissors, found objects (cardboard, aluminum foil, pieces of plastic, etc.)

If project is to take place in a space other than your classroom:

- **Other spaces to be used:**
- **Appropriate planning with school staff:** N/A

Notes: Procure a large table to put in back of room for collection/ storage of found objects/materials

---

MULTIPLE INTELLIGENCES APPLICATIONS

Check all that will be included in the project.

- _X_ Linguistic
- _X_ Logical/Mathematical
- ___ Musical
- ___ Bodily/Kinesthetic
- _X_ Visual/Spatial
- ___ Naturalist
- _X_ Interpersonal
- _X_ Intrapersonal

BLOOM'S TAXONOMY APPLICATIONS

Check all that will be included in the project.

- _X_ Create
- _X_ Evaluate
- _X_ Analyze
- _X_ Apply
- _X_ Understand
- _X_ Remember

New Vocabulary (Minimum of Ten New Words) and Review of Learned Vocabulary: *Math:* square, triangle, rectangle, hexagon, polygon, trapezoid, estimate/approximate, 2-D, 3-D, length, height, depth, area, capacity, units, concave, convex, edge, face, vertices. *Visual Art:* analyze, observe, interpret, choice

Assessment Methods: Formative assessment will be employed throughout the process. As part of the opening discussion, students' basic understanding of the content will be assessed and the lesson plans will be adjusted to meet the needs of the students. Ongoing review of students' work will allow for the tailoring of the lesson plan, with additional coaching provided to students in need. Continual discussion at the end of each session will give the students the opportunity to review new content as well as to express their degree of understanding. In addition to the students' final presentation of their work, an end-of-unit test will be administered in keeping with district directives.

Collaborative Session One

Date/Time:

Aim of the Lesson: Introduction and explanation of project and materials to be used.

The Plan: Students will create and organize the structure of their notebooks utilizing a variety of measuring tools and pencils/markers to number pages and measure and block in areas for Title Page, Table of Contents, Brainstorming Chart, Vocabulary, Data, and Learning Diary, etc.

Activities Between Sessions One and Two

Date/Time:

Aim of the Lesson: To introduce the concept of geometric shapes and the difference in dimensional objects.

The Plan: Students will refer to the textbook. A video will be shown to reinforce understanding, with continual discussion to insure that all students are engaged. They will write what they have learned in the LD section of their journals.

Collaborative Session Two

Date/Time:

Aim of the Lesson: To learn to recognize different geometric shapes.

The Plan: Using attached format, brainstorm on white board: "What do we know about measuring stuff?" Organize students' prior knowledge by having students circle words that fit into the same category of measure with the same color of dry-erase pen. Students then transfer information to brainstorm chart, glue in book's appropriate page and add to Table of Contents.

Activities Between Sessions Two and Three

Date/Time:

Aim of the Lesson: To reinforce recognition and measurement of geometric shapes.

The Plan: With students working in small teams, review previous material by asking students to name shapes projected on a screen. Teams are given time to go to the white board to collaboratively draw the answer to different questions as well as spell the names of the particular shapes. (Weather permitting, this will be done outdoors in the picnic area using chart paper instead of the white board.)

Collaborative Session Three

Date/Time:

Aim of the Lesson: Continue to learn different geometric shapes and begin to measure the objects they create.

The Plan: Students color and cut geometric shapes printed on handout. In journal, title each page with the name of shape and glue shape to appropriate page in book. Record in Table of Contents. On each shape, number each side from one to three, four, or five; measure and record findings in standard and metric measure, in book next to shape. Add up sides to get perimeter and record in notebook.

Activities Between Sessions Three and Four

Date/Time:

Aim of the Lesson: To recognize, draw, and manipulate different geometric shapes. Students are encouraged to decorate the shapes, using colors and designs that portray their personalities.

The Plan: Create a study of each shape in their journal by creating collages, using different colors of the shape and different techniques such as, layering, overlapping, mosaic, quilting etc. After session eight, each student picks a favorite design to use on the cover of the notebook.

Collaborative Session Four

Date/Time:

Aim of the Lesson: To create and manipulate geometric shapes using printed templates.

The Plan: On regular paper, precisely color and cut 3-D shape patterns for various sized triangular prisms, rectangular prisms, and cubes. Using a ruler, students fold precisely on lines to create 3-D shapes. Glue the bottom side of each 3-D shape into notebook so when flattened it will be within the outer edges of the book page but when popped-up will recreate the 3-D shape. Outline the shape while flat, measure, and record length of each side of outline.

Activities Between Sessions Four and Five

Date/Time:

Aim of the Lesson: More time for the activities described in "Activities Between Sessions Three and Four."

The Plan: Students continue work to reinforce their ability to recognize, draw, and manipulate different shapes.

Collaborative Session Five

Date/Time:

Aim of the Lesson: "Catch Up and Look Up"

The Plan: To ensure that all students have completed the previous parts of the project, students choose to work alone or with a buddy to complete the previous activities. If they are completed, students can go to the computer stations to watch the animated video supporting the content. Encourage students to observe different geometric shapes in art, architecture, fabric art, and furnishings. Have them write these observations in their journal and, if possible, attach a photograph, drawing or cut-out as part of the journal entry.

Activities Between Sessions Five and Six

Date/Time:

Aim of the Lesson: To reinforce recognizing, drawing, and manipulating different geometric shapes.

The Plan: Create a study of each shape (in the book on the adjacent page) by creating collages using different colors of the shape and different techniques such as, layering, overlapping, mosaic, quilting, etc. After Session Eight, each student picks a favorite design to use on the cover of the notebook. Continue to encourage students to observe different geometric shapes in art, architecture, fabric art, and furnishing. Have students study *After All* (Charles Demuth, American, 1883–1935), and discuss the use of geometric shapes in the oil painting. Have them write these observations in their journal and, if possible, attach a photograph, interpretive drawings or cutout as part of the journal entry.

Collaborative Session Six

Date/Time:

Aim of the Lesson: To learn the definition of 3-D by creating 3-D shapes.

The Plan: Using the patterns from the previous lesson, students use cardstock paper to make the 3-D shapes. Instead of gluing them in their notebook, they tape shapes together, leaving one side as open access to the inside. Each student should have three different 3-D shapes.

Activities Between Sessions Six and Seven

Date/Time:

Aim of the Lesson: More time for the activities described in "Activities Between Sessions Five and Six."

The Plan: Continue as in previous session.

Collaborative Session Seven

Date/Time:

Aim of the Lesson: To continue understanding 3-D shapes through manipulation and measuring them.

The Plan: Create widgets to measure the capacity of previously created 3-D shapes. Each student will create six miniature triangular prisms and six miniature cubes to become widgets. Each group of students can share widgets to measure and record the capacity of their shapes. Continue discussion of observed geometric shapes in architecture, etc.

Activities Between Sessions Seven and Eight

Date/Time:

Aim of the Lesson: To recognize, draw, and manipulate different geometric shapes.

The Plan: Create a study of each shape (in the book on the adjacent page) by creating collages using different colors of the shape and different techniques such as, layering, overlapping, mosaic, quilting, etc. After session eight, each student picks a favorite design to use on the cover of the notebook. At this point, students may work in small groups to discuss and compare their work, making suggestions for the final product.

Collaborative Session Eight

Date/Time:

Aim of the Lesson: Really thinking outside the box: Creating the "nonbox."

The Plan: Students assess found pieces of cardboard, plastic, foil, etc., and use pre-set amounts (the shape must fit on the student desk) to create "nontraditional," solid 3-D shapes. Students determine methods to measure and record perimeter of sides and area of shapes. Continue discussion of observed geometric shapes in architecture, etc.

Activities Between Sessions Eight and Nine

Date/Time:

Aim of the Lesson: **To reinforce the recognizing, drawing, and manipulating of different geometric shapes.**

The Plan: Students choose their favorite shapes and create the cover for their notebook. For homework, the students are to reflect on the meanings of their choices for color and design and then write a short description, which will become the inside front cover. The writing sample will have proper sentence structure, spelling, and punctuation. After review by the teacher, the students will work at a computer station to enter the description into a word processing program, print it, cut it out, and paste onto the inside front cover.

Collaborative Session Nine

Date/Time:

Aim of the Lesson: "Catch Up"

The Plan: Students are directed to complete the creation of nonstandard shapes and their measurements. They will work individually or with a buddy. Students who have completed the project will be encouraged to help a fellow student who is not finished. Students will also be able to complete the work on their covers and inside front covers. Continue discussion of observed geometric shapes in architecture, etc.

Activities Between Sessions Nine and Ten

Date/Time:

Aim of the Lesson: "Wrap-Up, Test-Up"

The Plan: After a short introduction, students complete a short, formal written test (district standard). After the test, students discuss how they wish to explain and display their final products, including their journals and different shapes and their documentation of geometric shapes in art, architecture, etc.

Collaborative Session Ten

Date/Time:

Aim of the Lesson: A final review of the entire project.

The Plan: Individually, students briefly describe to the rest of the class and to a visiting class what they learned and what they liked about the project. They display their journals and their "out of the box" creations, as well as explain their observations of geometric shapes in art and architecture, etc.

BRAINSTORMING CHART—What Do We Know About Measuring?							
What We Measure ➜ **How We Measure** ⬇	**Weight**	**Time**	**Temperature**	**Length**	**Capacity**	**Angles**	**Money**
	pound	minute	Fahrenheit	inch	cup	right	penny
	ton	day	Celsius	centimeter	liter		dollar
	gram	hour		meter	pint		quarter
	kilogram	second		foot	quart		nickel
	ounce	year		yard	gallon		dime
	carat	month		mile			half dollar
		week		kilometer			euro
Total number of answers	6	7	2	7	5	1	7

The **Mode** is the number that occurs most often in a set of numbers. What is the Mode of the totals? __7__

The **Range** is the difference between the highest and lowest number in a set of numbers. What is the Range? __6__

The **Mean** can be found by adding all the numbers and dividing the sum by the number of addends. What is the Mean? __5__

The **Median** is the middle value of a set of numbers. What is the Median? __6__

Source: Adapted from a lesson plan by Teaching Artist Tracy Rosof-Petersen, Lake Worth, Florida.

Sample Geometric Templates for Lesson

These are reduced-size examples of the templates you can use for the 2-D and 3-D shapes. Full-size versions can be found in various elementary grade materials.

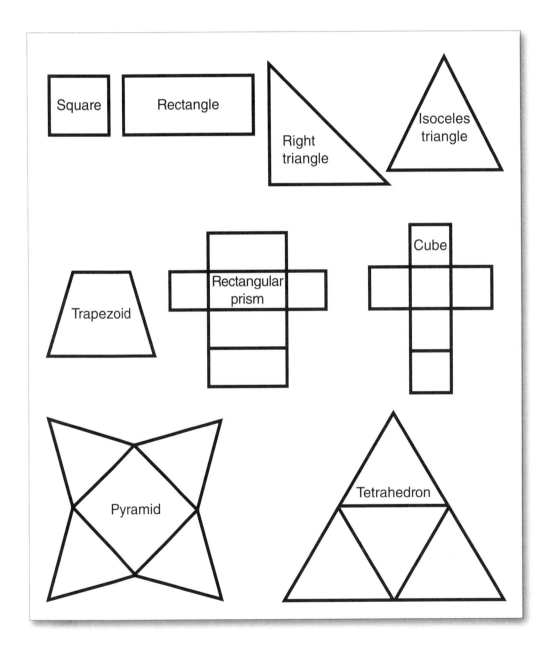

Sample Intermediate Grades Arts-Integration Lesson Plan Format

Two Collaborating Teachers or Teacher With Teaching Artist

The "Big Idea"—Main Topic or Theme: _____

_____

Objective of the Arts-Integrated Project: _____

_____

Plan Created By: _____

Assisted By: _____

Primary Curriculum Subject: _____

    Benchmarks: _____

_____

Integrated Curriculum Subjects: _____

    Benchmarks: _____

_____

Primary Art Form: _____

    Benchmarks: _____

_____

Integrated Art Forms: _____

    Benchmarks: _____

_____

Planning Responsibilities
List the responsibilities of each teacher and/or teaching artist
with due dates to keep everyone on schedule.

NAME:

RESPONSIBILITY(IES) AND DUE DATES:

NAME:

RESPONSIBILITY(IES) AND DUE DATES:

NAME:

RESPONSIBILITY(IES) AND DUE DATES:

NAME:

RESPONSIBILITY(IES) AND DUE DATES:

Three Essential Questions (Comprehension):

EQ 1: _____

Bloom's Application: _____

EQ 2: _____

Bloom's Application: _____

EQ 3: _____

Bloom's Application: _____

Management Planning

Schedule

- Number of Sessions: _____
- Length of Sessions: _____
- Specific Dates/Times: _____

Materials Needed: _____

If project is to take place in a space other than your classroom:

- Other Spaces to Be Used:
- Appropriate Planning With School Staff:

Notes:

MULTIPLE INTELLIGENCES APPLICATIONS

Check all that will be included in the project.

____ Linguistic

____ Logical/Mathematical

____ Musical

____ Bodily/Kinesthetic

____ Visual/Spatial

____ Naturalist

____ Interpersonal

____ Intrapersonal

BLOOM'S TAXONOMY APPLICATIONS

Check all that will be included in the project.

____ Create

____ Evaluate

____ Analyze

____ Apply

____ Understand

____ Remember

New Vocabulary (Minimum of Ten New Words):

Assessment Methods:

Collaborative Session One

Date/Time:

Aim of the Lesson:

The Plan:

Activities Between Sessions One and Two

Date/Time:

Aim of the Lesson:

The Plan:

WHAT'S COMING?

Perhaps the greatest challenges to integrating the arts into STEM lessons occur in high schools. With tighter schedules than middle schools, getting STEM and arts-area teachers to collaborate is no easy task. But it can be done. And we are pleased to relate that a number of schools are doing it. How? The next chapter offers suggestions gathered from current STEAM participants about how to find the time to create and implement successful STEAM lessons in high school.

Chapter 5—Implementing Arts Integration in the Intermediate Grades (5–8)

Major Points to Ponder

Jot down key points, ideas, strategies, and resources that you want to consider later.

_____

_____

_____

_____

_____

_____

_____

_____

_____

_____

_____

_____

_____

Chapter 6

Implementing Arts Integration in the High School Grades (9–12)

Oh, had I but followed the arts!

—William Shakespeare, *Twelfth Night*

Many things happen to the human brain as it passes from preadolescence to adolescence. During the years leading up to adolescence, the brain is making more neural connections than it really needs. This overabundance of unneeded connections can cause the brain to work less efficiently. To prevent this slowdown in performance, a pruning process called *apoptosis* begins around early adolescence. Just as a farmer removes the weak seedlings so the stronger ones can grow, the brain cuts back those connections that are no longer needed, allowing the remaining networks to work more efficiently and effectively. Meanwhile, as frontal lobe development continues, executive functions become more pronounced, and the individual starts acting more maturely. The brain begins to explore options and to assess the social implications before making a decision. That insufferable teenager is slowly becoming a more reasoned adult.

The potential for creative expression grows significantly during these years. Although their intellectual curiosity should be at an all-time high, their years in school have dulled it. Recall that this is where only 10 percent of high school students describe themselves as creative, down from 50 percent in the middle school years. All those "why" questions that these students asked in the elementary grades have turned to "Just tell me what I need to know." Fixed mind-sets are now running rampant, and this is a calamity of no small proportion! When a vast majority of students believe they are not creative, they are not going to attempt creative projects.

As cerebral networks expand in the frontal lobe, the brain's pattern-seeking capabilities are nearly fully functional, and the students' ability to make more abstract connections among related concepts improves dramatically. But will they get that opportunity in STEM classes? Apart from the obvious internal relationships among the STEM subjects—mathematics with science, for example—will they encounter activities that will help them make connections to the arts or other subject areas? Will they understand how scientific progress affected the economic and political history of our country and the world? Will they recognize the importance of acquiring competent language skills in order to be successful in mathematics and engineering? Will they explore the ways in which the arts have contributed to significant developments in the STEM areas? With STEM, probably not; with STEAM, yes! In this chapter, we will offer some examples of STEM lessons that are enhanced by arts-related activities to become STEAM lessons, providing the novelty and interest that are likely to attract and maintain student focus.

During these years, gross motor skills are becoming much more coordinated, so the adolescent feels more confident in activities involving movement. Music and dance now become important to this age group. Both are methods of expressing social identity and peer acceptance. Participating in team sports is common, but some students prefer individual activities, such as gymnastics and dance. All are improvisational and choreographed movements achieving a desired goal, whether it be winning a game or contest, or telling a story.

> *Music and dance now become important to this age group. Both are methods of expressing social identity and peer acceptance.*

The social brain is also maturing, so the need for peer acceptance drives students to spend more time with their peers and less with their family. Thus, peer relationships often become the adolescent's primary source of social support. Of course, some students are more socially mature than others. Some move among their peers with ease and confidence, while others are awkward and shy. Arts-related activities can encourage the less social students to interact meaningfully and positively with others, and to recognize the value and personal satisfaction of creating STEAM projects together.

STEAM AND THE CULTURE OF THE HIGH SCHOOL

Purposefully integrating arts-related skills into STEM classes in the high school is not an easy task because of the restraints of schedules and, in some cases, contractual issues. We believe, however, that STEM teachers, like their colleagues, want to do what is best for their students. If they recognize that introducing arts-related skills and topics into their classes could raise student interest and achievement, we assume they will at least consider this approach and our suggestions for turning STEM into STEAM. And that is more likely to occur if the notion of STEAM is compatible with the school's culture.

Generally, the culture of a school is reflected in its mission statement. Looking at the mission statements of public high schools across the United States, the following statements emerge in one form or another:

- To prepare them for college or a job during this critical transition period into adulthood (Chicago Public Schools)
- Students achieve their full potential and become productive members within their community (Dallas Public Schools).
- Strive for academic excellence while making school a fun environment in which to learn (Denver Public Schools)
- To provide a high-quality education that prepares, ensures, and empowers all students to achieve their full intellectual and social potential in order to become lifelong learners and productive members of society (Philadelphia Public Schools)
- To provide each student with an equal opportunity to succeed by promoting intellectual growth, creativity, self-discipline, cultural and linguistic sensitivity, democratic responsibility, economic competence, and physical and mental health so that each student can achieve his or her maximum potential (San Francisco Public Schools)

A survey of private and Catholic schools noted the following goals:

- To empower students who can effect positive change in society (Archdiocese of Philadelphia)
- To challenge all students according to their ability (Archdiocese of Philadelphia)

No matter whether public or private, schools exist in communities for the purpose of educating their youth. Preschool, elementary, and middle school mission statements are much simpler, where high school mission statements are built to specifically address that phase of life where "the insufferable teenager is slowly becoming a more reasoned adult." Many high school mission statements reflect the urban situation in which they are located, responding with very strong personal growth goals in contrast to the difficult situations around them. As students make their way and grow through these four years, school administrators, teachers, and parents and guardians often are barely a step ahead of this growth, always looking for the next strategy to help guide a teenager. High school is often the place where teenagers learn life skills from teachers and peers and where they make decisions as to how they will respond to challenges, successes, and failures. They begin to adopt lifestyle patterns that form their individual persona. Consequently, the culture of a high school can be critical in determining whether a student becomes a productive member of society. Fortunately, the power of arts education and arts-integrated instruction has been the key ingredient that has made high school a successful experience for otherwise struggling students.

Remembering the Purpose of High Schools

However noble mission statements may be, the true purpose of high school has always been to prepare students for life *after* high school. Granted, at the turn of the twentieth century, most high schools had entrance examinations that restricted admittance to about 5 percent of the population, and it prepared these selected students for college. By the early twentieth century, high schools moved toward open enrollment and offered more practical choices in curriculum, including vocational training and liberal arts courses of various descriptions. The goal became to prepare students for whatever they chose after they left high school—whether they graduated or not. College was not the option for everyone, so high school courses in practical sciences, basic mathematics, mechanical drawing, and home economics actually prepared non–college bound students for postschool employment and survival. The arts were flourishing, with almost every high school having a band, an orchestra, choruses, art classes, debate and rhetoric clubs, and annual dramatic productions.

In a small high school, there was tremendous overlapping in student opportunities simply because there were fewer students. The quarterback also played tuba in the orchestra, and the cheerleader was on the school newspaper staff and sang in the glee club. The arts were intertwined in everything not because there were studies and focus groups who determined this was important but because it was what worked. Early twentieth-century schools were integral parts of the community where the arts added cultural value to urban neighborhoods and to new suburban communities. As a result, that rich liberal arts education turned out successful, problem-solving adults who created an impressive national infrastructure that built the

> *Early twentieth-century schools were integral parts of the community where the arts added cultural value to urban neighborhoods and to new suburban communities.*

United States. Students who did go to college emerged as some of the greatest thinkers of the century and whose contributions to society are inestimable. Students who did not go to college but chose to build other careers, such as working in industry, became the economic backbone for the country with many creating very successful businesses that have continued to this day.

During the mid-twentieth century, getting students into college became the primary goal of a high school education. When the Soviet Union in October 1957 launched *Sputnik I,* the first artificial Earth satellite, the Western world was stunned that the Soviet space program was apparently well ahead of the U.S. program. President Eisenhower quickly signed the National Defense Education Act that encouraged students to go to college and study mathematics, science, and foreign languages with tuition paid by government grants or low-interest loans. National committees were established to produce model curriculums in the sciences and mathematics. These efforts led to a new emphasis on STEM in the nation's schools. "Who has time for the arts when the Soviets are winning the space race!" was the mantra of the time.

Much like the blob of those 1950s shocking black-and-white horror films, this dramatic change in educational goals and structure crept into the national culture, causing drastic changes in curriculum and allocation of resources. In the name of national security, local high schools were merged into mega-campuses, course offerings in high schools morphed into a college-centric format, and the art of high school teaching dramatically altered. Lecture became the primary instructional strategy because it allowed teachers to efficiently "cover the curriculum."

At the turn of the twenty-first century, the "blob" of these changes has depleted the number of opportunities for creative and innovative instruction because high-stakes testing—especially in literacy and numeracy—has become the main focus of many instructional decisions. Advanced placement courses and International Baccalaureate programs have grown, and the arts and other creative programs are waning due to the reallocation of resources and tightening budgets. School is becoming less meaningful for an increasing number of students. The National Center for Education Statistics reports that the current national average high school dropout rate is a discouraging 25 percent (Aud et al., 2011). Of those who do graduate, 30 percent do not go on to college right after graduation. How does this compare with other developed countries? In 2008, the U.S. high school graduation rate was lower than the rates of the United Kingdom, Switzerland, Norway, South Korea, Japan, Italy, Ireland, Germany, Finland, and Denmark (Organisation for Economic Co-operation and Development [OECD], 2011).

> *Forty-three percent of students who start college will not graduate in six years—that's right, six years.*

What about college? Forty-three percent of students who start college will not graduate in six years— that's right, *six* years. The United States once led the world in college graduates. Meanwhile, other nations have caught up, and some have pulled ahead, such as Australia, Belgium, Canada, Denmark, France, Ireland, Israel, Japan, South Korea, Luxembourg, New Zealand, Norway, Sweden, and the United Kingdom (OECD, 2011). Equally disturbing is a report from Complete College America (2012) that about 40 percent of those students who do go to college find themselves placed in freshman remedial courses in mathematics, reading, and writing because high school did not prepare these students for college-level work. That number is up from 33 percent in 2001.

Our purpose here is not to disparage high schools. Both authors have taught for years in high schools and are well aware of the dynamic influences that affect high school life. We know that teachers and students *want* to be successful, even though some of the factors affecting student success and achievement are beyond the reach of the school's faculty and administration. Rather, as we noted in the Introduction, STEM, as currently conceived, is apparently not living up to expectations. It has not yet been effective at improving student performance in the STEM areas nor is it narrowing the gender or minority gap in STEM achievement.

The Value of Grit

We believe we have presented in the preceding chapters ample evidence that integrating arts-related skills into the high school STEM curriculum is one way to make more students successful in these courses. Arts integration, by its very nature, is certain to stimulate creativity among STEM students. When these students are regularly exposed to the creative process, they recognize the importance of persistence—the need to keep on working until the task is done. Too often teachers hear students say, "Just give me the answer and let's move on."

> **When students are exposed to the creative process, they recognize the importance of persistence—the need to keep on working until the task is done. Add passion and you have grit!**

Schooling, through its shallow instruction and frequent fill-in-the-blank testing, has taught students to find the one correct answer and move on. They have not learned the value of persistence nor developed the passion to finish a task when other problems arise. This is not what science and mathematics are; nor is it how scientists, engineers, and mathematicians work.

Persistence is a far more important characteristic than many people think. In recent years, psychologists, such as Angela Duckworth of the University of Pennsylvania, have been studying the relationship between persistence and creative achievement (Duckworth, Peterson, Matthews, & Kelly, 2007). It turns out that having the passion and the ability to stick with a task is one of the most important predictors of success. This combination— passion plus persistence—is known as *grit,* and it explains a greater percentage of individual success than do intelligence and IQ scores. Duckworth has developed a scale to measure an individual's grit and has found that grit can compensate for talent. People who have high grit but average talent can be more successful and creative than those who have high talent but little grit. That is because the latter tend to give up when faced with obstacles while the former persevere to finish the task. Not surprisingly, one of Duckworth's studies revealed that beginning teachers with high grit scores were much more likely to remain in challenging, under-resourced schools than those with low grit scores. Teachers in these types of schools need to be creative in order to present dynamic and meaningful lessons with a limited amount of instructional supplies. They use their creativity to help students make models and posters and conduct science experiments with inexpensive materials.

As STEM becomes STEAM in more high schools, these students will benefit from increased exposure to the creative process, improve their own creativity, raise motivation, and strengthen their grit—characteristics that will not only make them more successful in STEM courses but in their other subject areas as well. Perhaps communities will then recognize the importance of retaining arts education not only as arts integration but also as stand-alone courses in the arts. Politicians, educational administrators, and those who decide what teachers must teach may discover what great educators have known all along: the arts are integral and life-giving to the process of learning and the art of living. If high school prepares students for life after high school, now more than ever, the active involvement in the arts throughout high school is necessary, and the STEAM classes may lead the way.

Arts Classes, Arts Integration, or Both?

Most high schools have some arts programming still available. However, in these large and often college-oriented campuses, the ability for many students to have some kind of authentic arts education is very difficult, especially when school budgets get tight. At best, students may get one semester of some kind of art or music once or twice in their high school experience. Dance and drama programs have almost ceased to exist. High school scheduling often limits opportunities for collaborative teaching experiences. Nonetheless, the prospects for arts-integrated programming are more frequent in high school than in primary or middle school. The key factor here is that high school students have the capability to work on their own with guidance and coaching from a teacher. With technology offering an abundance of arts information, high school students can do a significant amount of learning on their own and, in fact, many high school programs offer online instruction, much like colleges.

The Arts Show the Human Side of STEM

Teaching is an art and a science. Research in educational neuroscience can tell us how the brain learns best, thus providing teachers with the knowledge they need to plan the instructional strategies and learning environment that are most likely to result in student success. But the artistry comes in translating that plan into the dynamic performance and face-to-face instructional experiences that form the drama of the STEM lesson. Humans conveying knowledge and wisdom to younger humans is the foundation of all cultures. Successful high school teachers in all subjects present concepts and various sources of information so their students can become self-directed and creative learners. Creativity involves trial and error, making choices and decisions, and finally assessing the end product.

> **Humans conveying knowledge and wisdom to younger humans is the foundation of all cultures.**

Imagine actors working from a script, researching the time period of the piece, and then creating their character under the guidance of a director. The director leads the actors through a strenuous process that involves new knowledge, collaboration, self-reflection, evaluation, and presentation of the final work. The audience makes the ultimate judgment, and its feedback may require alterations to the script or staging to produce a better result. Now imagine student scientists following a similar pattern when pursuing a problem. They start with a hypothesis (script), research what is already known about the topic, and create an experiment under the guidance of a STEM teacher. They collaborate and reflect on their findings, which may require them to modify the experiment to get the final answer. Here are art and science working in tandem, as one creative mind. Technology, of course, can provide information, but it cannot provide the human interaction, support, and guidance so necessary for creativity to flourish.

Planning for an Arts-Integrated Lesson: Rerun or New Show?

We noted in Chapter 3 that teachers can find a comfortable instruction zone and mind-set and often do not realize that they are in a repetitive pattern, teaching content the same way year after year. By nature, humans prefer routine and shun change. Schoolteachers are not immune to this syndrome. One reason for this pattern is that high school teachers are completely departmentalized and seldom, if ever, need to delve into other curriculum areas. Ironically, one of the early purposes of departmentalization was so teachers would know their students over the course of three or four years, thus adapting their instructional strategies to reach each student. However, this was in the day when STEM subjects were all-inclusive. Today, mathematics, for example, is broken down into five to ten subtopics from Algebra I to Advanced Calculus, creating "specialists" out of teachers. The concept of departmental instruction has morphed into a "mini-college" operation. This format, combined with the grouping of students—either by student choice or administrative decision—creates a myopic instructional culture. Consequently, teachers often find themselves using the same instructional strategies over again and, sometimes, many years will pass before they even notice this pattern. It is time for exchanging instructional reruns for a new production. After all, good teaching involves great acting!

STEM to STEAM: One Teacher's Aha Moment

One of the authors recently met with a high school science teacher in suburban New Jersey. In the three-hour discussion, there was no mistaking that this is a dedicated, intelligent teacher who is passionate about his vocation and about how he teaches his freshman biology classes. Doing a random once-over of his lesson plans, the author honed in on a well-designed lesson plan about the structure of cells. It involved collaboration of students in groups, formative assessment, essential questions, and research—all great activities. The final reports/projects by the student groups ranged from fair to professional-quality PowerPoint presentations boasting outstanding design and presentation. Most students made excellent use of the Internet as they cut and pasted beautiful photos of cells in various forms. When asked what he thought of the project, he stated he thought it was average and had about the same results as in the past five years.

Upon reviewing the past five years of lesson plans for the same unit, he had clearly made changes based on student response, but all these changes were devoted to saving time and to having better online resources outlined for the students prior to the actual class. Although well prepared, this lesson plan was built around addressing the technological needs of the students. It helped those adept at computer programs to create bigger and better presentations, resulting in a range of presentations from fair to outstanding. Laboratory time was actually computer time with minimal hands-on laboratory. The teacher's input was primarily coaching students with the computer programs and not on the biology of cell structure. Students who were extremely computer savvy were on top of the game, an observation not lost on this teacher.

Finally, the author asked, "Did you ever consider having the students create models of cells out of clay?" And there was a classic "lightbulb" moment. (See the "Cell Creation" sample in Chapter 7.) The teacher immediately got it. He stated how obvious such a simple project could be, but it never occurred to him. More discussion revealed that a large arts program exists in the high school, and although there is no collaboration between the departments whatsoever, he knew a number of the art teachers and was sure he could set up a set of collaborative lessons. He recognized the power of STEAM and immediately made some educated choices in changing the lesson plans for the coming year.

PUSHING STEAM ALONG

Clearly, we encourage the collaboration of teachers, teaching artists, and artists as the most enriching experience for a teacher. Teachers not only learn new information and strategies but they can also begin to change their outlook on their own subject area, their students, and themselves. If you do get involved in these collaborations, a mind-set shake-up is sure to occur because the arts enrich everyone! Did you take the arts perception assessment in Chapter 3? Have you been able to reflect on your own personal artistic interests to see what connections can be made with your instructional strategies? For example, if you have an interest in rock music, you could use that to kick off a unit in a Physical Science class addressing the shift in frequency in sound or electromagnetic waves due to the relative motion of a source or receiver (FL Benchmark SC.912.P.10.21). You have their attention and, with little work, you can wrap an entire unit around rock music.

> *[When teachers collaborate, they] not only learn new information and strategies but they . . . change their outlook on their own subject area, their students, and themselves.*

We mentioned earlier that the potential for creative expression of students grows significantly during the high school years as the frontal lobe matures, yet so few of these students describe themselves as creative. Survey your STEM students, and find those who are interested in music, art, dance, drama, film, and technology. Here is an example of a simple survey you could administer that was developed by a visual arts high school teacher (Middleton, 2008). Adapt it as needed for your classes.

Sample Interest Survey for High School STEM Students

Name: _____ Period: _____

This survey is to help me get to know you better. You do not need to answer any question that makes you feel uncomfortable, but do answer as many as you can. Thank you.

1. Why did you select this class? _____

2. What do you like to do in your free time? _____

3. What type of music is your favorite? _____

4. Have you a parent or sibling working in an art-related field? _____ If so, what? _____

5. How often do you visit a museum or art gallery? _____

6. Have you ever taken any art classes? _____ If so, when? _____

7. Do you draw, sketch, or paint artwork on a regular basis? _____

8. Do you play a musical instrument? _____ If so, what? _____

9. Have you ever taken dance classes? _____ If so, when? _____ Do you still? _____

10. Have you ever gone to a professional dance performance? _____ How long ago? _____

11. Have you ever been to a professional play performance? _____ How long ago? _____

12. Have you recently acted in a play? _____ If so, when/where? _____ _____

13. How would you describe your interest in technology? _____

14. Check any of the following that you would be interested in doing:

   ___ Draw caricatures or cartoons.

   ___ Create a movie.

   ___ Visit an art museum.

   ___ Work as a writer at a magazine or newspaper.

   ___ Design houses and buildings.

   ___ Create and choreograph a dance that depicts some famous event.

   ___ Sculpt in clay.

   ___ Build a model out of cardboard or wood.

Source: Adapted from Middleton (2008) with permission of the author.

With this information, you could do things like arrange for a student interested in art to peer teach mathematics students the nontechnological drawing of conic sections (MA.9.1–2, 3). Encourage the actor to work with you to create a murder mystery using propositional logic, arguments, and methods of proof to find the culprit (MA.912.D.6.1–7). Engage a member of the "Save the Earth Club" to work with you in creating interactive lesson plans for the Earth Systems and Patterns unit (SC.912.E.7.1–9). The boy in the third desk who can't sit still needs interaction, not detention. That fidgeting boy is not necessarily disinterested in the topic; he needs to be actively engaged. The arts provide an unending source of interactive ways that will engage students, raise motivation, and support a growth mind-set. He could be your next student assistant. All these activities have another benefit: they encourage self-confidence, something that cannot really be taught.

SAMPLE COMPARISONS OF TRADITIONAL STEM AND ARTS-INTEGRATED STEAM LESSONS

Grades 9–12—SCIENCE
Big Idea: Diversity and Evolution of Living Organisms
Florida Benchmarks: SC.9.12.L.15.1, 15
Cognitive Complexity: Moderate to High

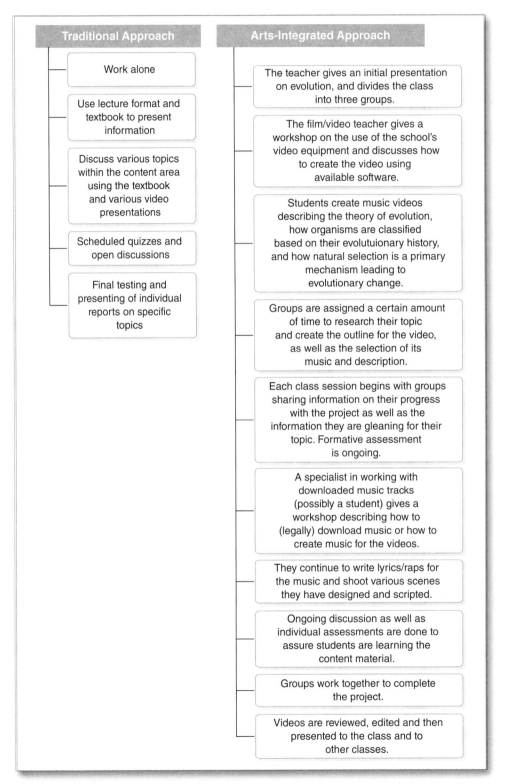

Traditional Approach	Arts-Integrated Approach
Work alone	The teacher gives an initial presentation on evolution, and divides the class into three groups.
Use lecture format and textbook to present information	The film/video teacher gives a workshop on the use of the school's video equipment and discusses how to create the video using available software.
Discuss various topics within the content area using the textbook and various video presentations	Students create music videos describing the theory of evolution, how organisms are classified based on their evolutuionary history, and how natural selection is a primary mechanism leading to evolutionary change.
Scheduled quizzes and open discussions	Groups are assigned a certain amount of time to research their topic and create the outline for the video, as well as the selection of its music and description.
Final testing and presenting of individual reports on specific topics	Each class session begins with groups sharing information on their progress with the project as well as the information they are gleaning for their topic. Formative assessment is ongoing.
	A specialist in working with downloaded music tracks (possibly a student) gives a workshop describing how to (legally) download music or how to create music for the videos.
	They continue to write lyrics/raps for the music and shoot various scenes they have designed and scripted.
	Ongoing discussion as well as individual assessments are done to assure students are learning the content material.
	Groups work together to complete the project.
	Videos are reviewed, edited and then presented to the class and to other classes.

Figure 6.1   Comparison of the traditional and arts-related approaches.

This is a common topic in high school biology courses. Perhaps because of the controversy surrounding this topic, it is often a teacher-centered presentation with lots of facts, photos, and videos. Students become passive observers. In the arts-integrated STEAM approach, students are actively engaged in the topic and develop a deep understanding of the origins and implications of biodiversity on our planet.

Note the major differences between these two approaches. The arts-integrated STEAM activities are student-centered and interesting, thereby raising student engagement and understanding. Formative assessments can be used along the way, followed by a variety of summative assessments—including performance assessments—when the unit is completed.

Here are two tested arts-integrated STEM units that have proven to be stimulating and creative experiences for tech-savvy high school students. The teacher, perhaps with student input, decides how simple or complex the unit should be. Both units require extensive time and can be carried out over several weeks while related classroom instruction continues.

Science (Biology)—Grades 9 to 12: "It's Alive!": Creating the Human Skeletal Form and Systems From Found Objects

High school students are media and movie junkies. They are surrounded by mythical games, worlds, and beings that can often defy description. Creatures that were once frightening have been given personalities and more important reasons for existing other than simply terrifying an audience. Young people have become somewhat immune to "shock value" and have actually embraced it and learned from it. They know the difference in blood types from the many new vampire films, and it didn't take a textbook. Let's work with that to produce an interesting, interactive, and creative unit on human anatomy and systems.

Curriculum Objectives:

- To define the major bones of the axial and appendicular skeleton and the histology of bone tissue
- To define and understand the anatomy and histology of muscle tissue
- To identify the major muscles of the human
- To identify and understand the functions of the spinal cord, the endocrine system, heart and cardiovascular system, the lymph system, the circulatory system, the respiratory system, the digestive system, and the nervous system

Artistic Objectives:

Visual Art:

- To demonstrate self-expression by integrating curiosity, range of interests, attentiveness, complexity, and artistic intention in the art-making process
- To identify rationales for aesthetic choices
- To assess the works of others, using established or derived criteria, and to support conclusions and judgments about artistic progress
- To use descriptive terms and varied approaches in art analysis to explain the meaning or purpose of an artwork

Social/Emotional Objectives:

- To become confident in making choices that require explanation and, at times, defense
- To collaborate in creating something that requires skills that might not be immediately apparent and supporting others in this journey

The Project: This is a long-range project that requires quite a bit of planning and scheduling; after all, we are building a human form. This project can be as simple as understanding the skeletal structure or as complex as including major markings (foramina, fossae, etc.), creating the central and peripheral nervous systems or using a simple garden fountain pump and quarter inch plastic tubing to demonstrate the circulatory system. This is where the Creative Process (see Chapter 2) is imperative. The "incubation stage" runs throughout this project. It can include three to five state standards or up to fifty-three. This is for you to decide. For the sake of variety, we have constructed this lesson plan in four modules, supporting the concept that the lesson plans in this book are meant to be altered and adapted to your particular situation. Each module is approximately one to three weeks, with about one day per week at the front of the project and three to five days per week toward the end of the project.

Activities:

MODULE 1: Using textbooks, lecture, and video, present the students with an overview of the systems and organs of the human body. Introduce them to the concept of creating art using found objects by doing research online and capturing images of the most interesting and different works of art. They are to document all work in a traditional notebook or by computer or iPad. Note-taking is continuous and students should keep a journal, just as scientists do. For a bit of fun, show the video clip from the movie "Young Frankenstein" where Dr. Frankenstein finally finds his grandfather's journals. It will not only entertain, but will bring home the importance of keeping detailed journals and notes.

MODULE 2: Ask the class to do research on "found object art" or "assemblage art," and make choices as to what art works interest them, and why. They also research the advantages of reclaiming and recycling materials. If possible, a local artist who specializes in such work can come in to explain the work and the process with examples. Explain and discuss the Creative Process (Chapter 2) with the class. Remind them to document all their research and opinions.

Divide the class into groups to decide how to "create" this humanoid. They will discuss what types of materials should be used for the bones (wood or PVC pipe?), what will represent muscle tissue (cushion foam that can be carved or papier mâché?), what will represent the major organs (a clock for the heart? recovered drain pipes and food cans for the digestive system? a conglomeration of found objects to create the brain, eyes, and ears?), and so on. The groups converge and decide what will be the best objects to use to create the humanoid. They should do preliminary drawings either in a traditional notebook or by computer, with descriptions of all materials and objects, including what bones and organs they represent, and how they will be connected and supported. (Note: This is where you need to have someone who is handy with simple power tools, such as a drill and saw, and simple nuts and bolts to lend a hand. The bones will need to move, and if you are not this power-tool person, convince a colleague to help.) Of course, be aware of all safety precautions. Hint: You might want to contact a local department store to have them donate a mannequin stand that can support the form. Meanwhile, the class is continually doing research as well as having typical in-class instruction related to the human systems.

MODULE 3: The class brings in the found objects, which are placed in boxes, categorized appropriately by systems, etc. Consider having a student or two create a computer-generated list to keep track of the parts. The students continue to work with partners or in small groups drawing the form. Ultimately, the students should be able to explain the function and purpose of each part and how it interacts with other parts.

MODULE 4: The class as a whole agrees on the final artistic depiction of the humanoid, and work begins on construction. Your organizational skills must be in high gear for this part, and do not forget to plan ahead for extra time for these exciting classes. You might need a double period here and there. You will want the students to work in groups of two to four; each group constructs one part of the form, such as an arm, a leg, or the torso. Once the components are constructed, the final assembly takes place and the supplementary components (tissue, organs, veins, etc.) are added. Again, the simplicity or complexity of this project is up to you.

Assessment: Students work individually or in pairs to describe particular parts and functions of the form. You can assess their notebooks in a portfolio format or whatever formula you use. You may also need to do traditional testing if that is required by your school or district.

Materials: Varied and uncategorized. Power drill, saw, nuts, bolts, picture wire, filament, and a glue gun

Multiple Intelligences Addressed: Visual/Spatial, Kinesthetic, Logical/Mathematical, Interpersonal, Intrapersonal, Naturalist

Bloom's Levels Addressed: Remembering, Understanding, Applying, Analyzing, Evaluating, Creating

Mathematics/Science—Grades 9 to 12: "Living Land": Designing and Building a Community Garden

Most schools have a "green component" at work in some form. It might be as simple as a recycling program or as complex as having the good fortune to be in a LEED (Leadership in Energy and Environmental Design) certified building. Whatever the case, this project can work in any scenario as long as there is some land or empty space available. In suburban and rural areas, a garden can be constructed in the ground, while in urban areas, the garden may need to be constructed above ground in planters. This is an excellent way to apply many mathematical concepts as well as incorporate many scientific and, of course, artistic and design elements.

Curriculum Objectives:

Mathematics:

- To apply and solve linear equations and inequalities in a real-world setting
- To apply geometric theory in a real-world setting

Science:

- To apply knowledge of ecology and earth-to-table concepts in a real-world setting
- To make planting choices based on local weather and conditions

Artistic Objectives:

Visual Art:

- To compare artwork, architecture, designs and/or models to understand how technical and utilitarian components impact aesthetic qualities as well as a local community

Social/Emotional Objectives:

- To actively participate in a project that not only affects the student but also the local community at large
- To work on a project that is long-term, requiring diligence and patience
- To learn and accept the divergence of different communities and their customs and culture
- To work collaboratively with fellow students as well as community members
- To gain a deeper respect for our environment

The Project: Community gardens, in all types of settings, abound throughout the world. Their designs and purposes are as varied as the communities in which they are located. This is a long-term project that will be planned according to your local climate. For the sake of organization, this lesson plan is divided into four parts. You may need to subdivide each part, flip some parts, or stretch a part across a full year depending on your local school schedule and weather conditions. Rely on your judgment, but try not to eliminate any of the parts because many of the activities are sequential. Consider coordinating with a local garden club or your local Extension Service as these folks offer a wealth of information and assistance.

This is yet another project that can be as small or as large as you wish, and once the students get started, our bet is that the latter will rule. This is a true integration project that, in the perfect world, would involve the collaboration of the math, science, social studies, and art teachers. The possibilities are endless, and the overall effect on the communities can be immeasurable.

Activities: Show the class a video or slides of various community gardens that exist throughout the world (available on Google Images). Ask the students to look for global cultural differences, and encourage them to observe various applications of linear equations (How was that step garden designed? What is the slope?), geometric shapes, artistic choices as well as the difference in the types of plantings that vary from garden to garden. Students will view this video a number of times; the aim is increasing their powers of observation and finding more applications as time goes on.

Students will keep either a traditional or electronic journal for all their work. For the design, you can purchase simple and inexpensive garden design software, which is the way to go for computer-based design. (There are also some very basic free programs available on the Internet.) These programs also offer a tremendous amount of mathematical applications that would be a great help to you and the class. You may decide to do both a traditional pencil and ruler method as well as a computer-generated method that will keep the students engaged.

PART 1: Present to the students the concepts of linear equations and inequalities, and show how they have real-world applications. Include geometric concepts, applications, and their representations with coordinate systems. All the while, you are reminding them of the gardens that they had viewed and encouraging them to look again for more applications of these mathematical concepts. Upon observing one of the gardens, they are encouraged to work backward and form an equation, for example, in a step garden (as in stair steps) they could eventually come up with the equation illustrated below, namely $y = (2/3) x - 4$.

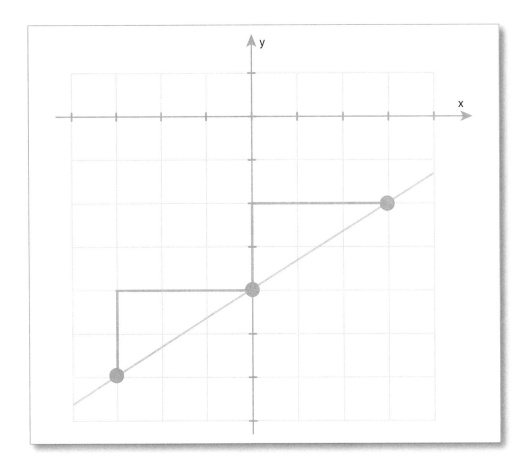

If possible, this is the time to bring in an expert to discuss the creation of the garden. This person will help you and the class to determine the best location and make suggestions and considerations for the design, in or above ground. You may want some students to graph the different possibilities and eventually graph the overall decisions of the class regarding the final product. Your expert will offer excellent advice about what types of soil, fertilizers, irrigation, and plant materials will work best to avoid a waste of time, money, and energy. The students will make planting choices and create a timeline or calendar depicting when the crops (should you plant a vegetable garden) can be harvested and used by the community.

Be sure to be in constant contact with those who manage the property where you work as they will be a critical ally throughout the process. Rely on them for understanding local building and environmental codes as well as safety, irrigation, and drainage issues.

PART 2: The class works in small groups to assess the area of the school or community property where the garden will be located. Using their notes from the guest lecture and the video observations, they begin to design the garden. While making artistic choices, remind them that mathematical and geometric operations must be employed. One author mentored such a project where the students created glazed pottery irrigation "sprinklers" that were not only visually stunning but completely functional for irrigation.

PART 3: The class works as a whole and makes collaborative decisions for the final design and installation. Here is the hitch: Every artistic choice for the construction, where applicable, will be supported by a mathematical or geometric equation or detailed drawing. These drawings and diagrams will eventually be printed individually and laminated or mounted and installed at various sections of the garden, effectively making it a living mathematics equation.

PART 4: The garden is completed with proper soil, organic fertilizers, and composting bins and is finally planted. Depending on your time and the involvement of your science and mathematics teachers, students may begin to monitor the growth of plantings, the required rates of watering, the use of composting, etc.

Assessment: This is the perfect formative assessment situation. As the students are creating their designs, they are also creating the mathematics and science to support it. Either it works or it doesn't. Thus the creative process kicks in and they, with your coaching, search for a Plan B if necessary. Use traditional testing as well if your school or local district requires it.

Materials: A compilation video of various community gardens from around the world (a month or two prior, assign this to two or three students who are masters of the video realm; the research will be fun, enlightening, and will create ownership), garden design software, appropriate wood, tools and hardware to create sections of the garden, permeable fabric for above-ground gardens, low-pressure irrigation system (available from home improvement stores and very easy to install from a simple faucet), soil, and mulch (available from recycling sites and from your local Extension Service), seeds, plants, and signage

Multiple Intelligences Addressed: Visual/Spatial, Kinesthetic, Logical/Mathematical, Interpersonal, Intrapersonal, Naturalist

Bloom's Levels Addressed: Remembering, Understanding, Applying, Analyzing, Evaluating, Creating

Other Activities that High School Teachers Have Tried

- Asking students to create a Rube Goldberg-type machine to demonstrate a food chain or web
- When studying sound, asking students to create their own musical instrument and to explain it and play it for the class
- Demonstrating the notion and motion of plate tectonics through song and dance
- Asking the students to use any artistic format to demonstrate or illustrate the water cycle
- Asking students to create a moving tableau (see Chapter 7) to represent dynamic equilibrium in a chemical reaction

These teachers have also mentioned that once they started adapting STEM lessons so they contained arts-related activities, their students began suggesting other ways to include the arts when learning STEM content. With your creativity and theirs, high school STEM lessons can become exciting and creative ventures that are more likely to keep students engaged while actually remembering what they have learned. What more could you ask for?

WHAT'S COMING?

The next step in the STEM to STEAM progression is to look at actual lesson plans that show the integration of arts into STEM subjects. For convenience, we have separated the sample lessons into two chapters. In the next chapter, we present some examples of STEAM lessons in science, technology, and engineering (STE) concepts. STEAM lessons in mathematics are in Chapter 8.

Chapter 6—Implementing Arts Integration in the High School Grades (9–12)

Major Points to Ponder

Jot down key points, ideas, strategies, and resources that you want to consider later.

_____

_____

_____

_____

_____

_____

_____

_____

_____

_____

_____

_____

_____

_____

_____

Chapter 7

STEAM Lesson Plan Appetizers in Science, Technology, and Engineering

The faculty of art is to change events; the faculty of science is to foresee them. The phenomena with which we deal are controlled by art; they are predicted by science.

—Henry Thomas Buckle, British Historian (1821–1862)

This chapter offers some additional ideas on ways to integrate arts-related activities and skills into lessons involving science, technology, and engineering (STE). Of course, in some cases, mathematics may be needed to complete the activity. We have not included separate activities for just engineering or technology because these areas are an integral part for the sample lessons. Activities focusing mainly on mathematics are in the next chapter. You can adapt any of these suggestions for use in a wide range of grade levels.

THE APPETIZERS

The lesson plan "appetizers" that follow are meant to be the beginning of a complete lesson plan, something to make you want to dive into the "full-course" of creating your own, tailor-made STEAM lesson plan. The ideas presented in these appetizers are the beginning of your creative journey. They are presented with suggested range of grade-level appropriateness, which will change with your needs for your own class and grade level. Look back on Chapter 2, and review the "Stages of Creative Thinking" and take time to prepare and especially to "incubate" your plan ideas. Using the suggested lesson plan formats at the ends of Chapters 4, 5, and 6 will help keep you on course. Keep the following notes in mind as you move forward:

- Benchmarks are not included in these appetizers because the exact benchmarks and codes vary from state to state. Remember that, in addition to the STEM benchmarks, you should include benchmarks for language arts, social studies, and any other curriculum area covered by your lesson plan. You also may have to follow specific lesson plan directives from your school or district. Make use of journaling as a creative writing exercise or as a way to improve your students' grammar and punctuation.
- The arts projects suggested here are by no means the only arts that can be incorporated. Remember to use your own creativity, bring in another teacher or teaching artist, and have fun coming up with new art projects to keep the students excited and engaged.
- The materials needed for your lesson can vary as much as you wish and will depend on what you have available. If you change the "seasoning" of the main course you are about to serve, because it tastes wonderful and the students eat it up, you have succeeded in creating a successful main course, and no one except you knows of the change.
- Scheduling is often a problem, so keep in mind that the activities need not happen in consecutive days. Just be sure that if there are more than two days between each activity, you create a "connecting activity" to keep the students' memories tweaked. The connecting activity does not need to be lengthy, and it could be as short as a brief discussion before lunch or while the students are lining up for dismissal.

Test your creativity, but have fun as well.

Science—Grade K:
"My World Through My Eyes"

Curriculum Objective:

- To learn that one can better learn about the world and the living things that surround us through careful observation

Artistic Objective:

- To explore basic structural elements of art, especially color

Social/Emotional Objectives:

- To generate ideas and images for artwork that communicate awareness of self

Activities: Students create a small fan book of primary and secondary colors, using index card stock and markers, water colors, tempera, or colored pencils. They color a predetermined number of cards and print the name of the color on the card. The cards are then stapled together to form the fan book. Students are taken on a "tour" of the property around the school building or of the block where the school is located. They are guided to observe the many colors that exist in nature and in the buildings around them. Using their fan books, they determine how many of their colors can be found. You encourage the students to decide what colors they liked the best and why and how important it is to take time to observe things carefully. They also discuss how the various colors made them feel, such as the light green of the new leaves on a tree or the dingy brown of an abandoned building. Finally, the students make freehand drawings of the image(s) they liked or remember most from the tour, including a drawing of themselves, using colors that describe how they felt. Continually coach the students to be creative and reflective.

Assessment: The students' final drawings will show their levels of observation abilities as well as their sense of self.

Materials: Index cards, crayons, markers, tempera, colored pencils, drawing paper, and a stapler

Multiple Intelligences Addressed: Linguistic, Visual/Spatial, Interpersonal, Intrapersonal, Naturalist

Bloom's Levels Addressed: Remembering, Understanding, Applying, Analyzing, Evaluating, Creating

Science—Grades 1 to 5: Habitat

Curriculum Objectives:

- To understand the natural world through habitat models
- To recognize the interdependence of living organisms through careful observation

Artistic Objectives:

- To create four different habitat models by displaying the landscape, including indigenous plants and animals, and using gathered and recycled materials
- To understand and create collages for the landscape background, the floor, and the clay plants and animals

Social/Emotional Objectives:

- To work cooperatively and independently
- To develop fine motor skills
- To follow step-by-step modeling instructions and become comfortable with "do overs"

Activities: Start by asking the students to brainstorm each habitat's components, including landscape, weather, and indigenous plants and animals. Students make a collage of the landscape backdrop by cutting and pasting magazine pictures onto construction and art papers. They make a collage of the landscape's floor using modeling clay and natural and recycled materials. They can create plants out of modeling clay. At some point the students should discuss the plant life of each habitat as well as the indigenous animals and their predator/prey role.

Assessment: Writing in daily journals, formative assessment, and required district/school testing.

Materials: Cardboard flats, magazines, construction and art papers, duct tape, gathered natural materials, recycled materials, scissors, glue, modeling clay

Multiple Intelligences Addressed: Linguistic, Logical/Mathematical, Bodily/Kinesthetic, Visual/Spatial, Interpersonal, Intrapersonal, Naturalist

Bloom's Levels Addressed: Remembering, Understanding, Applying, Analyzing, Evaluating, Creating

Science—Grades 1 to 8:
Earth to Table

This is a long-range activity that can be adapted for multiple grade levels and can be as simple or as complex as your students can handle. It involves growing a garden, and it includes some basic food preparation techniques, using simple recipes. The students can not only make these dishes at school as part of the project but can also bring them home to share with family and friends. Another creative option for this project is to have students paint twelve-inch by twelve-inch cement pavers, each in the style of a famous artist. Be sure to use exterior paint and to seal the pavers appropriately before and after painting them.

This is an extensive project, but schools that have done it report remarkable student engagement, no matter what grade levels are involved. It has wonderful social and personal growth outcomes that are not mentioned here. It also has many challenges associated with those desirable outcomes. This project can excite you and the students to get out of the classroom, away from those grow-lights, and put your hands into the earth.

Curriculum Objectives:

- To learn that food is a basic need
- To observe how the energy from the sun transfers to growing plants
- To understand the interaction of humans and animals with plant life
- To learn how a garden can transform part of a yard and a neighborhood as well as lifestyles

Benchmarks Note: In addition to the obvious science benchmarks, you may also be able to include benchmarks for physical education and social studies that might not appear in your state's science benchmarks.

Artistic Objectives:

- To design the planting areas using paper, pencils, and colored markers
- To create plant marker signs
- To create painted tile or cement block walkways (if appropriate)

Social Emotional Objectives:

- To work collaboratively
- To learn how to make choices as a group for the good of the overall community
- To learn how being outdoors and working in the earth can be calming and focusing

Activities: Start with a session that discusses options for healthy eating, including what is and is not good food and where food comes from. All of the discussions and class progress is charted on white boards as well as in the students' personal journals. These journals include drawings, cutouts, collages, and any other artistic formats supporting the project.

Students create an herb and vegetable garden, either in or above ground. This is where assistance from a master gardener, your local Extension Service, or botanical garden is immensely helpful because there is a science to gardening. Initial planning must include collaboration with whoever manages your school's facilities to ensure a safe location that is accessible on weekends and holidays for watering and weeding. Your school district may even be able to help you in clearing a space for an in-ground garden or securing a space for an above-ground garden.

This project involves long-term planning because a carrot does not grow in five class sessions. Clever use of time will allow you to make this a full-year project, with possible continuation over the summer months when classes are not in session. You may also want to invite parents, local retirees, and friends to assist in the project.

Assessment: This project calls for formative assessment. Depending on your local curriculum, you may also need to include standard assessment and testing. It is important to include the students' journal writings and drawings, verbal presentations and discussions, and your observations of the hands-on parts of the project as part of assessing what they know, understand, and can do.

Materials: This is by no means a complete list, as that will vary with complexity of the project:

- Classroom: Journals, colored pencils, crayons, and markers, rulers, glue sticks, gardening and nature magazines, text book, and video background information
- The Garden: Seeds, plant stakes, twine, stakes, and markers for plants, top soil, compost, and appropriate fertilizers, typical garden tools, chicken wire fencing to protect plants from intruding animals, and hoses for watering. You can water a small plot (four feet by four feet) by hand with a watering can or bucket, but anything larger requires a hose with a near-by faucet. The raised and above ground planters will require appropriate lumber (four inch by four-inch posts, one-inch by six-inch boards), screws, power tools, and a person who has basic understanding of do-it-yourself projects. All materials will depend on the final design and size of your garden. There are also biodegradable planters available at many online gardening sites.

Multiple Intelligences Addressed: Linguistic, Logical/Mathematical, Bodily/Kinesthetic, Visual/Spatial, Interpersonal, Intrapersonal, Naturalist

Bloom's Levels Addressed: Remembering, Understanding, Applying, Analyzing, Evaluating, Creating

Science—Grades 3 to 9: Digest-a-Fabric

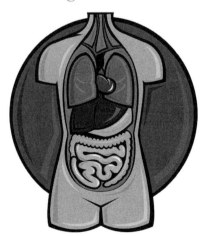

This series of lessons is similar to a dry dissection in that the students learn, draw, and cut out the body parts involved in human digestion. You can make this as simple (Grades 3–5) or as complex (Grades 6–9) as you wish. If you use background music, it should be free of lyrics so as to facilitate the students work rather than distract them.

Curriculum Objective:

- To learn about the digestive system and how it functions within the human body
- To learn the capabilities of online research and how to use this information ethically

Artistic Objectives:

- To view different uses of fabric from classic quilting to fashion design and discuss colors and textures and why the artists or designers may have made the choices they did
- To identify the artistic process and apply it to a specific scientific topic
- To examine and revise artwork throughout the art-making process to refine the work and achieve a personal artistic objective
- To assess one's work and the work of others using derived criteria to support choices made in the artistic process

Social/Emotional Objectives:

In learning and appreciating the process of making art, students learn the following:

- To recognize that there is more than one way to solve a problem, and that different artists make difference choices
- To share ideas and collaborate to solve a particular artistic challenge, thus understanding the value of collegiality and teamwork

Activities: Students learn about the digestive system and the important part it plays in the human body. After briefly identifying the parts of the system, such as mouth, epiglottis, esophagus, liver, gallbladder, stomach, pancreas, small intestine, large intestine, and appendix, the students work in pairs using print material or online research to create individual folders containing their research. In each pair, one student lays on his/her back, arms at the sides, on top of about four feet of brown kraft paper, while the second student traces the outline of the other's body from neck to knees. Together they cut the kraft paper into the body shape. Having students choose music to be playing in the background can add a fun element to the project.

The pair discusses the size and shape of the digestive organs and draws them free-hand on leftover kraft paper (or any other available paper) to create a pattern. They then choose a fabric to represent the organ based on the actual color of the organ or make an artistic choice for an overall look of the project. They pin the drawn pattern to the fabric, cut it out, and glue it to the paper body form. Each digestive organ is appropriately labeled. As each organ is created, the students research online (or in available print materials) and create a folder with this information.

Assessment: Students will be able to verbally explain the digestive system and how it functions and label its parts. A short textbook test is part of the final evaluation.

Materials: Various fabric scraps, large roll of brown kraft paper, pencils, markers, paste, quilting pins (if appropriate) and glue, heavy card stock for labels, access to a computer and printer

Multiple Intelligences Addressed: Visual/Spatial, Kinesthetic, Logical/Mathematical, Interpersonal, Intrapersonal, Naturalist

Bloom's Levels Addressed: Remembering, Understanding, Applying, Analyzing, Evaluating, Creating

(Note: This lesson is adapted from Teaching Artist Tracy Rosof-Petersen, Lake Worth, Florida.)

Science—Grades 3 to 9:
Learning Pitch/Frequency With a Bottle Xylophone

Many of us remember how the pitch of a sound made by tapping a glass of water changes when one changes the water level. This activity introduces music as a means of learning about pitch/frequency. You can make the activity as simple or as complex as you like, depending on the grade and interest level of your students.

Curriculum Objectives:

- To understand the concept of pitch/frequency
- To recognize the factors that can affect pitch/frequency
- To recognize how changes in pitch/frequency can produce difference musical notes and chords

Artistic Objectives:

- To learn to play a simple song on the "xylophone" made of glass bottles
- To appreciate how the same musical tone can vary, depending on the instrument

Social/Emotional Objectives:

- To work cooperatively with peers to design and make a water-bottle xylophone

Activities: Depending on the grade level, the students can make a xylophone consisting of five to eight bottles (full octave). Many simple elementary-grade songs can be played with a five-note xylophone. The project is a bit easier for younger students if the bottles are all the same size (of course, no beer or liquor bottles permitted). It becomes more of a challenge with bottles of varying sizes. Students work as a class or in small groups and add water to one bottle as the starting note. Use a pitch pipe to verify the note's pitch. Free pitch pipe apps are available for cell phones. Metal and wooden spoons make fine mallets, and they produce different tones. Students then add water to other bottles to make a five- or eight-note xylophone. Songs such as "Oh, Susanna," "Row, Row, Row Your Boat," and "When the Saints Go Marching In" are fairly easy for younger students to learn. More challenging songs are "Darling Clementine," Beethoven's

Ode to Joy, and "Home on the Range." Older students can discover other songs to play.

If the bottles are identical, ask students to measure and record the height of the water in each bottle. Putting a cap on the bottle will prevent the water from evaporating if you plan to keep the xylophones for more than one lesson. Students discuss the project, including what they learned about sound and how the water level affects the pitch/frequency. They can play their songs for other classes. Several groups can tune their xylophones so they can play duets. Ask the class to research what other musical instruments might work on the same principle as the glass-bottle xylophone.

Materials: Glass bottles (same or various sizes, labels removed), water, metal and wooden spoons, bottle caps, pitch pipe

Multiple Intelligences Addressed: Linguistic, Logical/Mathematical, Musical, Kinesthetic, Visual/Spatial, Interpersonal, Intrapersonal

Bloom's Levels Addressed: Remembering, Understanding, Applying, Analyzing, Evaluating, Creating

Science—Grades 3 to 12: Using Drama in Science Lessons

Drama involves creative movement and role-playing, and can turn an otherwise plain lesson into a motivating and productive learning experience. David Kener (2012), a former drama teacher, suggests how teachers in all subject areas can use drama to enliven their lessons. Here are a few of his strategies that we have adapted so they would be appropriate for STE lessons. You can also alter, as needed, for different grade levels and student interest.

Curriculum Objectives:

- To use movement and drama activities to review and learn about various concepts and people in STE
- To develop observation and questioning skills
- To enhance student creativity through challenging and interesting activities

Artistic Objective:

- To understand how drama activities can enhance the study of STE concepts
- To recognize how purposeful movement can improve learning and retention of STE concepts

Social/Emotional Objectives:

- To recognize how collaboration with others can improve progress toward a learning goal
- To understand how using drama activities involving emotion can raise interest and enhance learning

Activities: Kener suggests several different types of activities to introduce drama into lessons.

1. **Spectrogram:** This is a movement exercise that samples the student's knowledge or opinion about a certain topic. It is an excellent way to check how much the students learned and retained from a previous lesson. The teacher informs the students that the room is divided into three sections identified as "yes," "no," and "not sure" and points to them. As the teacher asks a question, the students move to the section of the classroom that reflects their depth of understanding of the answer. The questions should move from simple to more complex. The students move to their section in silence as discussion is done later. The final question can be (1) the most difficult, (2) most provocative, or (3) the one that gets most closely to the ultimate learning objectives that you would like them to master. For example, a final question in a series of questions on weather could be, "Who knows the major factors that affect daily weather changes?" or "Who believes that the notion of global warming is a hoax?"

Once students move to answer this final question, there will be two or three distinct groups who share the same opinion. Ask the students in each group to discuss their points of view, and select a representative who will summarize their discussion. For older students, you could ask them to play the role of a character. In this example, it might be a particular political figure, a scientist or other stakeholder (see "hot-seating" in the following pages). You could also suggest that students switch roles at least once during the exercise in order to understand a different perspective—one of the major goals of role-playing.

2. **Tableau:** In this activity, the teacher gives each group of students either a STE concept that they have already studied or a new concept that has not yet been covered in class. The teacher can give the same concept to all groups or a different concept to each group. Each group works collaboratively to decide how to best represent the concept as a tableau. They must focus not just on representing the concept but also pay attention to their poses, facial expressions, and gestures. The tableau does not have to be static or silent, so movement and dialogue are permitted. Sound effects and music are also allowed.

   After the groups have had some research and rehearsal time, each group presents its scene to the class. Later, the students discuss what concept they believe the tableau represented. Students in the tableau share their research with the class and explain what choices they made when deciding how to present the tableau. As an added feature, one student could play the role of a reporter and interview members of the tableau. The teacher and class could also decide to video-record each tableau.

   Possible STE topics for the tableau:

   - Discovery of the Higg's boson
   - Discovery of the DNA structure
   - Story of an invention
   - Biological systems and processes
   - Chemical systems and reactions
   - Climate change
   - Designing and building a structure

3. **Hot-seating:** This is a role-playing activity that is useful when discussing the life and contributions of a famous scientist, engineer, or

technology wizard. Think of it as an interview on a current national talk show. A student assumes the role of a famous individual and sits in front of a group or the entire class. Students ask questions about the character's background, motivation, and work. In some instances, like the Wright brothers or DNA discoverers Watson and Crick, more than one character can be in the hot seat. When in the hot seat, the student(s) must answer the questions in character, using what they have learned about the famous individual. This activity lends a human element to the sciences by helping students realize that STE discoveries and advances are made by real people.

Assessment: Use formative assessments throughout the project. When completed, students should be able to discuss what they learned from the drama activities.

Materials: Will vary with the tableaus that the students choose

Multiple Intelligences Addressed: Visual/Spatial, Kinesthetic, Logical/ Mathematical, Interpersonal, Intrapersonal

Bloom's Levels Addressed: Remembering, Understanding, Applying, Analyzing, Evaluating, Creating

Science—Grades 5 to 9: "Cell Creation"

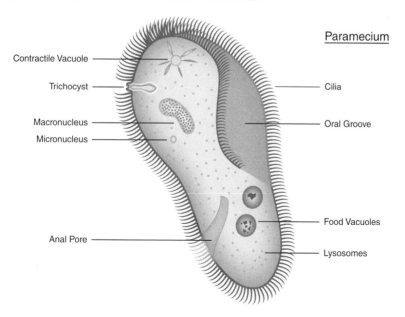

Paramecium

Contractile Vacuole

Trichocyst

Macronucleus

Micronucleus

Cilia

Oral Groove

Anal Pore

Food Vacuoles

Lysosomes

This activity gives students a chance to work with clay or similar materials to build cells. It is popular with students because many have never had the opportunity to use this medium in science classes. Beginner-level students work with modeling clay whereas older students can work with a ready-to-use, self-hardening clay that can be painted.

Curriculum Objectives:

- To learn the parts of plant and animal cells
- To understand how similar cells are organized to form structures in plants and animals

Artistic Objectives:

- To observe different sculptures via video and print and identify solutions for 3-D structural problems
- To identify the artistic process and apply it to a specific scientific topic
- To examine, revise, and refine artwork throughout the art-making process and achieve a personal artistic objective.
- To introduce or review color theory in order to mix modeling clay and paints to achieve appropriate colors

Social/Emotional Objectives:

In learning and appreciating the process of making art, students learn the following:

- To recognize that there is more than one way to solve a problem and that different artists make different choices
- To share ideas and collaborate to solve a particular artistic challenge, thus learning the value of collegiality and teamwork

Activities: Students learn the characteristics of plant and animal cells and, working in pairs, create models of the cells by pressing the clay onto a paper plate and creating parts of plant and animal cells from other clay, paying attention to appropriate colors and texture. After models have dried (and painted, if necessary), students label each part of the cell with a description.

Assessment: Students verbally describe the parts of the cells and how cells work. They will create questions that they ask each other to reinforce their knowledge and concepts.

Materials: Beginner: modeling clay in various colors, paper plates, wood tools; More Advanced: ready-to-use, self-hardening, and paintable modeling clay, tempera paints, and various size brushes

Multiple Intelligences Addressed: Visual/Spatial, Kinesthetic, Logical/ Mathematical, Interpersonal, Intrapersonal, Naturalist

Bloom's Levels Addressed: Remembering, Understanding, Applying, Analyzing, Evaluating, Creating

(Note: This lesson is adapted from Teaching Artist Tracy Rosof-Petersen, Lake Worth, Florida.)

Science—Grades 5 to 9: Using Mobiles to Teach About Levers

This lesson is an interesting way to show the application of levers to artistic work. In this case, it involves viewing the mobiles created by American sculptor Alexander Calder (1898–1976). Calder worked as a mechanical engineer before turning to sculpture and is considered the originator of the mobile. The activity covers several science, mathematics, and visual art standards (Ewald & Gerlman, 2010).

Curriculum Objectives:

- To understand the parts, functions, and three types of levers
- To be able to differentiate between potential and kinetic energy
- To study and interpret some of the mobiles created by Alexander Calder
- To build and manage a simple mobile

Artistic Objective:

- To understand how artists use scientific principles in creating their work

Social/Emotional Objective:

- To work collaboratively with other students to produce a work of art

Activities: Provide a review of previous information about simple machines and potential and kinetic energy. Explain the parts of a lever and the three types. Ask students to work in pairs and investigate the three types of levers and how they are used in the real world. Give some information about Alexander Calder, and project or display images of some of his mobiles. Explain to students that Calder's mobiles were informed and inspired by his knowledge of physics, mathematical concepts, the cosmos, and astronomy. Before Calder enrolled in art school, he had received his mechanical engineering degree, a decision influenced by his fascination with construction and mechanical apparatuses and machines.

Ask students to discuss mobiles as an art form and to describe what they like or dislike about Calder's work, and why. Ask students to research Calder's life and work. Explain to students that Calder's mobiles were informed and inspired by his knowledge of physics, mathematical concepts, and astronomy.

Using a ruler, string, and small paper cups, the students construct a mobile, either in small groups or as a class. (Add more art to the activity by using different colored strings and cups.) They place small objects in the cups to balance the mobile's arms. When finished, they discuss how they solved the problem of finding proper balance and what they noticed about changing the length of the strings supporting the cups, altering the weight loads, and changing the position of the fulcrum.

Assessment: Formative assessment as the project progresses and a summative test of your choice when it is completed

Materials: Rulers, string, small paper cups, small objects for balancing arms

Multiple Intelligences Addressed: Visual/Spatial, Kinesthetic, Logical/Mathematical, Interpersonal, Intrapersonal

Bloom's Levels Addressed: Remembering, Understanding, Applying, Analyzing, Evaluating, Creating

(Note: This lesson is adapted from Ewald & Gerlman [2010]. ARTSEDGE and The John F. Kennedy Center for Performing Arts. Adapted with permission.)

Science—Grades 6 to 12: "Born This Way"

Middle school and high school students are very familiar with this hit song. It will certainly be novel to introduce it into your unit on DNA. The lyrics get the message across about the extent to which DNA makes us who we are.

Curriculum Objectives:

- To experience the process of scientific inquiry and understand that it is a multifaceted activity
- To understand that scientific knowledge is durable and robust, but open to change
- To further understand the process of DNA replication, cell theory, and how life is maintained by various physiological functions essential for growth and reproduction

Artistic Objectives:

Music:

- To experiment with, and compare and perform, a variety of vocal styles and ensembles

- To evaluate and make appropriate adjustments to personal performance
- To evaluate one's own or another's compositions or improvisations and generate improvements individually or collaboratively

Theater:

- To collaborate with a team to outline several possibilities for the design of a performance

Dance:

- To analyze movement from varying perspectives, and to experiment with a variety of creative solutions to solve technical or choreographic challenges

Social/Emotional Objectives:

- To become confident in making choices that affect their "image" while learning to accept the personality differences and talents of others
- To work on production challenges together that will necessitate the blending of all talents for success

Activities: Students learn or review the concept of DNA, what it is, how it works, and why it is important in making us who we are. This can be done with lecture, textbook, video, or all of the above. The class listens to Lady Gaga's "Born This Way" with the actual lyrics printed on handouts. The project is to replace the original lyrics with lyrics describing facets and facts about DNA and to stage the final production using a karaoke track with movement and costume pieces. There are several ways to do this: (1) Divide the class into groups of four to six students and have each group write, create, and perform the number. (2) Organize "creative teams" with one working on lyrics, one on movement, one on design, and one to perform the number.

Assessment: Students take notes on their research and record in their journals what they are doing artistically and what connection that choice has regarding the content area. If possible, the final production could be filmed and shown to other classes. A written test could also be used.

Materials: Recording of "Born This Way" and appropriate audio equipment, a karaoke version (without lyrics, just accompaniment) of "Born This Way," costume pieces and materials that may be needed to make costume pieces and props

Multiple Intelligences Addressed: Visual/Spatial, Kinesthetic, Logical/Mathematical, Interpersonal, Intrapersonal, Naturalist, Musical

Bloom's Levels Addressed: Remembering, Understanding, Applying, Analyzing, Evaluating, Creating

Science—Grades 9 to 12: "The Case of the Origins of Life": Sherlock Holmes' "Bigger Than Life" Case!

Many students have seen the recent Sherlock Holmes films that are filled with intrigue, clever situations, and comedy. Latch on to this and use the format to your advantage as a means to investigate the somewhat sensitive topic of the origins of life on Earth.

Curriculum Objective:

- To describe the scientific explanations of the origin of life on Earth

Artistic Objectives:

- To create, refine, and sustain complex and believable characters for performance through the integration and application of artistic choices based on research

Social/Emotional Objectives:

- To use personal reflection to bring deeper understanding of the scientific knowledge regarding the origins of life, as well as a respect for the beliefs of others on the subject

Activities: After a brief class presentation of the basic content dealing with the origins of life (textbook and other materials particular to your situation), ask the students to create a play or a film with a Sherlock Holmes theme. This is where partnering with a fellow teacher in drama and/or film production is very useful. The idea is that Holmes and Watson have a client who comes to them with a mystery to solve: "What is the origin of life on earth?" The entire class begins to brainstorm ideas that will add intrigue to the story line, such as having only twenty-four hours to solve the case or something dismal or amazing will occur. (Students are rarely at a loss for such phenomenal ideas.) They analyze the information contained in their texts, and the class divides into smaller groups, each taking a strand of information and beginning to create a story line around it. This investigation, of course, can go in many directions, but they all must arrive at the same solution to the case with this famous line: "Elementary, my dear Watson." Depending on class interest, group sizes, and time available, this project can be structured in many different variations from very simple readings of the script or story lines to costumed performances or short videos.

Assessment: Continual review of student writings and discussions will afford you the information to know how to coach the students in the proper direction. Completed projects (scripts, plays, videos) will indicate understanding of the concepts. Written tests, assessments, portfolios, and journaling are also appropriate.

Materials: Basic background information from text or online, whatever is appropriate to your situation. Copies of Sherlock Holmes films (you can use the recent ones with Robert Downey Jr. as Sherlock, or the 1990s films, starring Jeremy Brett) with the homework assignment that students get together at their homes to view the films in small groups; computers, laptops, and other devices for the writing the scripts; costumes, video cameras, editing equipment, and whatever else is needed for your particular version of this project.

Multiple Intelligences Addressed: Linguistic, Logical/Mathematical, Musical, Bodily/ Kinesthetic, Visual/Spatial, Interpersonal, Intrapersonal, Naturalist

Bloom's Levels Addressed: Remembering, Understanding, Applying, Analyzing, Evaluating, Creating

Science—Grades 9 to 12: Earth Structures Described Through Mime and Theater

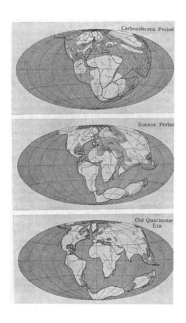

Discussing the large forces that cause tectonic movements as well as their structures and forces is often not a very exciting unit because of the obvious limits on student engagement. This motivating activity is a novel way to introduce this topic because it gets students involved by practicing mime. It takes a little extra planning, but teachers who have done this activity report superb student participation and achievement of the learning objectives. Should your students really get into this activity, you can make it more theatrical by using layers of stretched ten-foot fabric pieces to create bands indicating the layers of the earth. This makes it fun and maybe instead of saying, "Oh, maybe you are going too far," you may be saying, "You haven't gone far enough."

Curriculum Objectives:

- To understand that the scientific theory of plate tectonics provides a framework for much of modern geology
- To recognize that internal and external sources of energy have continuously altered the features of Earth by means of both constructive and destructive forces
- To understand that all life, including human civilization, is dependent on Earth's internal and external energy and material resources

Artistic Objectives:

- To understand the art of mime and physical theater by studying videos of famous performers such as Marcel Marceau, Charlie Chaplin, and Buster Keaton
- To create simple props and costumes to assist in the telling of the story
- To learn the history and techniques of theatrical makeup for use in mime
- To experience the process of telling a story without the use of one's voice
- To experience both interviewing and being interviewed on camera

Social/Emotional Objectives:

- To develop a deeper interpersonal understanding by looking at emotions from a different point of view and using these emotions in making a point nonverbally
- To be comfortable in using one's entire body in telling a story (not being afraid to look "different" or "funny")

Activities: Present the science content material using lecture, textbooks, and video. The class as a whole views portions of films that contain mime and discuss how it is done, how they as an audience might have varying interpretations of the action on the screen, and the differences between a comedic (Chaplin) and a more serious (Marceau) performance. Ask the students to take notes about costuming, props, and makeup for use in their own performances. If you have a mime artist in the area, now would be a good time to call that person for assistance.

The creation of mime takes a bit of coaching by the teacher. Here is where you take advantage of the "actors" in your class and ask for their help. The class is divided into groups of no more than five, and each group is assigned a topic to describe in mime, such as the different layers of the earth, the results of moving plates, geologic developments in your area of the country, and the effects of energy production and potential future consequences on the earth's structure. This will take a few classes and it would be wise to discuss the steps of creative thinking found in Chapter 2 with your class. You want them to learn to *incubate* their ideas, change their minds many times until the *illumination* of the "aha" moment happens. The members of each group share their creative ideas and engage in constructive criticism to hone their ability to observe dramatic movement. The final production is the presentation of describing physical interpretations of earth structures and forces through mime. You may wish to video-record these presentations and put them on DVDs as souvenirs of the project.

Assessment: Consider asking a student in your class who is into video production to conduct interviews of each group with a set of questions you create that center on the learning objectives. This is done as an "on the street" interview format. If the students can discuss and correctly answer the questions, the mime strategy was a success. You may need to use a written test or other format, as well.

Materials: Simple costume pieces, simple props created from available art materials and found objects, video camera, DVDs for recording mime performances.

Multiple Intelligences Addressed: Linguistic, Logical/Mathematical, Musical, Bodily/Kinesthetic, Visual/Spatial, Interpersonal, Intrapersonal, Naturalist

Bloom's Levels Addressed: Remembering, Understanding, Applying, Analyzing, Evaluating, Creating

Science—Grades 9 to 12:
Learning About Nature Through Watercolor

This activity gets students outside the classroom to observe nature and to represent natural objects in watercolor. This is much like the work of the French-American naturalist, John James Audubon (1785–1851), a self-taught artist who studied the natural world and created beautifully detailed paintings of birds in their natural habitat. Here, the students follow in Audubon's footsteps by creating naturalist paintings of plants.

Curriculum Objectives:

- To observe the natural world, especially plants
- To observe and record plant structures in detail

Artistic Objectives:

- To create a watercolor painting of a natural object
- To learn the techniques of using watercolor

Social/Emotional Objective:

- To share the watercolor with peers and to explain what was learned

Activities: Give each student watercolor paper and take the class for a walk to an outside area with plants and trees. Ask the students to observe the natural world around them and to note plants that attract their interest. Because they are going to record the characteristics of the plant in watercolor, they should select a specimen that has stems, leaves, flowers, bulbs, and roots intact, if possible. Once they find a specimen, they should sit down to draw it or, if possible, carefully uproot it and take it back to the classroom. If neither is possible, they can take a close-up picture of it with a digital camera.

On their watercolor paper, they should record their name, date, where they observed the plant, and its classification. After taking some time to study the plant's structures, they should block out its general shape using a soft pencil. Remind them to be observant and to take in all the details, such as veins in the leaves, markings on the flowers, and hairs or thorns on the stems and branches. They should draw the plant as they see it, rather than what they expect to see. Next is the watercolor (or colored pencils, if you prefer). They color in from lightest to darkest and should avoid using black. It is not necessary to color the entire drawing. When the painting is dry, the students can discuss—as a class or in groups—what they learned about their plant and how they felt about drawing it.

Assessment: The students can critique their own drawings and discuss what they would do differently the next time they draw a natural object.

Materials: Watercolor paper, soft pencils, natural specimen to draw, watercolors (or colored pencils), containers for water, and brushes

Multiple Intelligences Addressed: Linguistic, Bodily/Kinesthetic, Visual/Spatial, Interpersonal, Intrapersonal, Naturalist

Bloom's Levels Addressed: Remembering, Understanding, Applying, Analyzing, Evaluating, Creating

WHAT'S COMING?

Perhaps no major curriculum area in secondary schools is as unloved as mathematics. No one speaks of "science anxiety" or "social studies anxiety," but "math anxiety" is a common expression in many schools. When surveyed, students reveal numerous reasons for dreading mathematics, and this dread usually leads to low achievement (Sousa, 2008). Integrating the arts into mathematics lessons helps students to recognize the practical and real-world applications of mathematical concepts. The next chapter offers some sample STEAM lessons for mathematics in the hope that teachers may encourage their students to find new meaning and wonder in mathematics.

Chapter 7—STEAM Lesson Plan Appetizers in Science, Technology, and Engineering

Major Points to Ponder

Jot down key points, ideas, strategies, and resources that you want to consider later.

_____

_____

_____

_____

_____

_____

_____

_____

_____

_____

_____

_____

Chapter 8

STEAM Lesson Plan Appetizers in Mathematics

Math is about patterns, and patterns are what life is all about.

—Keith Devlin, *The Math Gene*

Secondary school students often say they have a difficult time with mathematics because they fail to see how mathematics relates to their real world. It doesn't even occur to them that all the electronic gadgets they use could never have been made without the mathematics included in their design and operation. Nature itself is incredibly mathematical. Just look at the symmetrical patterns that exist in our natural environment. For example, patterns exist in the markings of animals such as zebras and leopards, in snowflakes, and in the distinctive songs of birds. Spiders construct geometric webs of various patterns while bees build hexagonal cells in their honeycombs. The Fibonacci spiral is a pattern evident in pinecones, pineapples, and snail shells.

Integrating arts-related skills and activities into mathematics lessons, therefore, gives teachers the opportunity to show the applications of mathematics to nature and to many human endeavors, such as the arts. For example, music can be considered the artistic expression of mathematics. Timing, rhythm, frequency, and harmony are all dependent on mathematical relationships. In this chapter, you will find what we call "appetizers"—additional ideas on ways to integrate arts-related activities and skills into mathematics lessons. You can adapt any of these suggestions for use in a wide range of grade levels.

THE APPETIZERS

The lesson plan appetizers in mathematics that follow are meant to be the beginning of a complete lesson plan, something to make you want to dive into while creating your own, tailor-made arts-integrated lesson plan. The ideas presented in these appetizers are the beginning of your creative journey. They are presented with suggested range of grade-level appropriateness, which will change with your needs for your own class and grade level. Look back on Chapter 2, and review the "Stages of Creative Thinking"; take time to prepare and especially to "incubate" your plan ideas. Using the suggested lesson plan formats at the ends of Chapters 4, 5, and 6 will help keep you on course. Here are some points to keep in mind.

- Benchmarks are not included in these appetizers because the exact benchmarks and codes vary from state to state. Remember that, in addition to the STEM benchmarks, you should include benchmarks for language arts, social studies, and any other curriculum area covered by your lesson plan. You also may have to follow specific lesson plan directives from your school or district. Make use of journaling as a creative writing exercise or as a way to improve your students' grammar and punctuation.
- The arts projects suggested here are by no means the only arts that can be incorporated. Remember to use your own creativity, bring in another teacher or teaching artist, and have fun coming up with new art projects to keep the students excited and engaged.
- The materials needed for your lesson can vary as much as you wish and will depend on what you have available. If you change the "seasoning" of the main course you are about to serve—because it tastes

wonderful and the students eat it up—you have succeeded in creating a successful main course, and no one except you knows of the change.

- Scheduling is often a problem so keep in mind that the activities need not happen in consecutive days. Just be sure that if there are more than two days between each activity, you create a "connecting activity" to keep the students' memories tweaked. The connecting activity does not need to be lengthy, and it could be a short as a brief discussion before lunch, or while the students are lining up for dismissal.

Test your creativity, but have fun as well.

Mathematics—Grades 2 to 3: "Oceans of Time"

This is an effective unit, but creating the pieces for this project is time consuming. Plan ahead, and on one of those days when you and the students need a break, get out the paper, scissors, and crayons and cut out fish, while calming ocean sounds and music play in the background. You'll have most of the material prepared before the project begins.

Curriculum Objectives:

- To identify time to the nearest hour and half hour using both a regular clock and a digital clock
- To reinforce understanding of fractions half and quarter
- To reinforce the terms *to* and *after* as well as understanding numerical terms such as 3:25

Artistic Objectives:

- To reinforce gross and fine motor skills using rulers, yardsticks, and scissors
- To make color choices by mixing primary colors to create new colors that have a nautical feel and look

Social/Emotional Objectives:

- To learn the importance of time and how "being on time" is important in many situations
- To work collaboratively in small groups

Activities: Students create two types of clocks. The round clock faces will be created from large brown kraft paper that is about three to six feet wide. You will want to put sixty, 2-inch marks (use a large marker) around the clock face circumference indicating the minutes, as well as the numbers one through twelve. Students then create and cut out eight pie shapes representing a quarter of the circle and four representing a half of the circle. You can purchase precut foam fish, cut out and decorate "personal fish" (each child has three or four fish that they design), or if available, use real seashells that you might want the students to paint and personalize. Whatever you decide, you need sixty of them, representing sixty minutes. Using heavier stock paper, students create the hour and minute clock hands. Why not have a seahorse on the end of the minute hand and a mermaid on the hour hand?

Create the digital clock taking a double thickness of kraft paper and folding it into an oblong shape, about two feet wide and ten inches high, with a three-inch "pocket" folded up on the bottom of the rectangle that will hold numerical cards. The sides of the rectangle pocket should be secured with tape or staples so that the pocket can hold the cards. Students either cut or use precut (recommended) large index-sized cards, at least five inches by six inches. The hour cards are of one color while the minute cards are of another. While reviewing sequential counting with the entire class, one or two students use large markers to put one number on each card. The number fifteen, for example, con- sists of two cards, one with the number one and one with the number five. Be sure that you have enough numbers to represent such times as

12:45 and 10:15, remembering that these times require four cards each, one for each number. Once the number cards are created, each student can personalize them.

The objective now is to have the students become fluid in reading time from both types of clocks, while reinforcing their understanding of fractions. Students gather around the clock face, which is on the floor, and the digital "clock," which is on an easel, with the other pieces placed strategically on the outside of the circle. Beginning with a simple time, such as 3:00, choose students to put the clock hands correctly on the clock and the appropriate numbers into the digital clock pocket. Using a time such as 5:30, students use the clock hands and the digital clock numbers as before. However, they also decide what "pie pieces" to place on the clock to indicate the half hour and how many of the fish (or sea shells) to place on top of the pie pieces to indicate the number of minutes. This is a back-and-forth lesson between the two types of clocks, using the pie pieces and fish to reinforce how many minutes are in an hour, a half hour, and quarter hour. While doing so, you are continually referencing fraction concepts. Interwoven in this lesson is the use of the words "to" and "after" as in "quarter to two" or "twenty after ten." The students have personally bought into the project by creating it, and a very difficult lesson in telling time two ways is fun and successful. Incidentally, save all of these materials for when you have a lesson in fractions or a science class about the ocean.

Assessment: This is formative assessment in action. You will know the students learned the objective when they correctly identify the time. This is a very verbal exercise, so you may want to use assessments suggested in your textbook or other methods, as well.

Materials: Large kraft paper, pencils, rulers, yardsticks, paints, tape, stapler, and seashells if available

Multiple Intelligences Addressed: Linguistic, Logical/Mathematical, Bodily/Kinesthetic, Visual/Spatial, Interpersonal, Intrapersonal, Naturalist

Bloom's Levels Addressed: Remembering, Understanding, Applying, Analyzing, Evaluating, Creating

Mathematics—Grades 3 to 12: Using Drama in Mathematics Lessons

Drama involves creative movement and role-playing and can turn an otherwise plain lesson into a motivating and productive learning experience. David Kener (2012), a former drama teacher, suggests how teachers in all subject areas can use drama to enliven their lessons. Here are a few of his strategies that we have adapted so they would be appropriate for mathematics lessons. You can also alter, as needed, for different grade levels and student interest.

Curriculum Objective:

- To use movement and drama activities to review and learn about various concepts and people in mathematics
- To develop observation and questioning skills
- To enhance student creativity through challenging and interesting activities

Artistic Objective:

- To understand how drama activities can enhance the study of concepts in mathematics

- To recognize how purposeful movement can improve learning and retention of concepts in mathematics

Social/Emotional Objectives:

- To recognize how collaboration with others can improve progress toward a learning goal
- To understand how using drama activities involving emotion can raise interest and enhance learning

Activities: Kener suggests several different types of activities to introduce drama into lessons.

1. **Spectrogram:** This is a movement exercise that samples the students' knowledge or opinion about a certain topic. It is an excellent way to check how much the students learned and retained from a previous lesson. The teacher informs the students that the room is divided into three sections identified as "yes," "no," and "not sure" and points to them. As the teacher asks a question, the students move to the section of the classroom that reflects their depth of understanding of the answer. The questions should move from simple to more complex. The students move to their section in silence as discussion is done later. The final question can be (1) the most difficult, (2) most provocative, or (3) the one that gets most closely to the ultimate learning objectives that you would like them to master. For example, a final question in a series of questions on the Fibonacci spiral could be "Who knows where we can find examples of the Fibonacci spiral in nature" or "Who has a unique application of the Fibonacci spiral?"

   Once students move to answer this final question, there will be two or three distinct groups who share the same opinion. Ask the students in each group to discuss their points of view, and select a representative who will summarize their discussion. For older students, you could ask them to play the role of a character. In this example, it might be a particular political figure, a scientist, or other stakeholder (see "hot-seating" in the following pages). You could also suggest that students switch roles at least once during the exercise in order to understand a different perspective—one of the major goals of role-playing.

2. **Tableau:** In this activity, the teacher gives each group of students either a mathematics concept that they have already studied or a new concept that has not yet been covered in class. The teacher can give the same concept to all groups or a different concept to each group. Each group works collaboratively to decide how to best represent the concept as a tableau. They must focus not just on representing the concept but also pay attention to their poses, facial expressions, and gestures. The tableau does not have to be static or silent, so movement and dialogue are permitted. Sound effects and music are also allowed.

    After the groups have had some research and rehearsal time, each group presents its scene to the class. Later, the students discuss what concept they believe the tableau represented. Students in the tableau share their research with the class and explain what choices they made when deciding how to present the tableau. As an added feature, one student could play the role of a reporter and interview members of the tableau. The teacher and class could also decide to video-record each tableau.

    Possible mathematics topics for the tableau:

    - Development of the Fibonacci spiral
    - Designing and building the pyramids in Egypt
    - Story of a discovery or invention that required mathematics

3. **Hot-seating:** This is a role-playing activity that is useful when discussing the life and contributions of a famous mathematician. Think of it as an interview on a current national talk show. A student assumes the role of a famous individual and sits in front of a group or the entire class. Students ask questions about the character's background, motivation, and work. In some instances, more than one character can be in the hot seat. When in the hot seat, the student(s) must answer the questions in character, using what they have learned about the famous individual. This activity lends a human element to mathematics by helping students realize that discoveries and advances in mathematics are made by real people.

Assessment: Use formative assessments throughout the project. When completed, students should be able to discuss what they learned from the drama activities.

Materials: Will vary with the tableaus that the students choose

Multiple Intelligences Addressed: Visual/Spatial, Kinesthetic, Logical/ Mathematical, Interpersonal, Intrapersonal

Bloom's Levels Addressed: Remembering, Understanding, Applying, Analyzing, Evaluating, Creating

Mathematics—Grades 3 to 6: Introducing Artists in Mathematics Lessons

Curriculum Objectives:

- To enhance students' ability to use rulers to make geometric shapes

Artistic Objectives:

- To introduce or review their understanding of primary colors
- To gain an understanding of the work of various artists

Social/Emotional Objectives:

- To understand how artists use different geometric designs so their paintings evoke emotions
- To recognize how different people can have distinctly different feelings about the same painting

Activities: Show some examples of the work of painters who use geometric designs in their work. Examples are Dutch painters, Piet Mondrian (1872–1944) and Theo van Doesburg (1883–1931), whose works in their later years focused on geometric patterns and primary colors. (Note: Make sure that the students recognize that the primary colors for projected light are red, green, and blue, while the primary pigment colors among artists are red, yellow, and blue; although cyan, yellow, and magenta are also used.) A more contemporary geometric painter is American Roy Newell (1914–2006). Ask the class to do some research on the painters you introduced, and follow that with a class discussion of similarities and differences in these painters' works, especially the use of primary colors. After that discussion, have them draw horizontal and vertical lines on white paper with a ruler and to go over the lines with a black marker. They can then fill in some of their geometric rectangles with their choice of colors, using colored markers, paints, or crayons, leaving some white (negative) spaces.

Depending on the grade level and student interest, you can ask students to discuss in groups or with the class why they chose their particular design and color scheme. You could also ask them to discuss what importance mathematics has to artistic design. Ask if they have seen such applications in their home or in the community. Students can sign their work and display them in the class or on the school bulletin boards.

A further expansion of this lesson would be to ask students to investigate the work of another Dutch artist, M. C. Escher (1898–1972), known for his incongruous drawings and perspectives. After their research, the students discuss how Escher incorporated mathematics and symmetry into his works.

Assessment: Ask students what criteria they would use to judge their own work.

Materials: White paper; crayons, paints, or markers in various colors

Multiple Intelligences Addressed: Visual/Spatial, Kinesthetic, Logical/Mathematical, Interpersonal, Intrapersonal

Bloom's Levels Addressed: Remembering, Understanding, Applying, Analyzing, Evaluating, Creating

Mathematics—Grades 6 to 8: "Fave Films and Probability"

Probability is about prediction, but it may not be an interesting topic to most middle school students unless they see applications to the real world. What better application than movies! In this activity, students discuss in groups a recent movie they have all seen to determine what factors could have helped them predict the film's ending. This always proves to be a motiving activity, but discussions can quickly drift away from the main learning objectives. Therefore, you will want to give specific directives and prompts to the entire class, and then wander around, checking in on each group and coaching them to stay on task.

Curriculum Objectives:

- To understand the concept of probability by determining, comparing, and making predictions based on independent or dependent events
- To understand the importance of careful observation of details

Artistic Objective:

- To learn how to view a film and the many aspects of film making, in particular the story line, script, and character development and the importance of a film score (background music)

Social/Emotional Objective:

- To understand the difference between "acted" emotions that are seen in films and on reality TV shows and real emotions, and how to make choices in expressing their own emotions

Activities: Through discussion, determine what films the class has viewed in the past month or so, and chart them to determine which five or six films were the favorites. (Be sure to check your school's or district's guidelines regarding which types of movies can be discussed or shown.) Divide the class into groups based the films they have seen. Try to keep the groups no larger than six students. Each group will discuss the one film they have seen in common.

Ask the groups to start the discussion with the obvious: what they liked and didn't like about the film, their favorite character, their favorite scene, etc. Then, have the groups work backward from the end of the film and chart whatever actions, dialogue, and background music predicted the final out-come. Just as important, they determine what action and dialogue did *not* offer any clue to the film's outcome.

Each group prepares a report to the entire class, describing the factors in the film that enabled a prediction of the end of the film. They may use charts, white boards, standing display boards, and PowerPoint—whatever works for them and for you. Finally, discuss the process of predicting an outcome and make the application to mathematical problems, noting the importance of observing all details, and know which to disregard.

Assessment: This is formative assessment in action. This is a very verbal exercise so you may want to use assessments suggested in your textbook or other paper-and-pencil methods. You may also have them solve a math prob-lem on probability to determine the learning crossover.

Materials: Notebooks, chart paper, markers

Multiple Intelligences Addressed: Linguistic, Logical/Mathematical, Bodily/Kinesthetic, Visual/Spatial, Interpersonal, Intrapersonal

Bloom's Levels Addressed: Remembering, Understanding, Applying, Analyzing, Evaluating, Creating

Mathematics—Grades 9 to 12: Using Fibonacci to Make Memorable Music

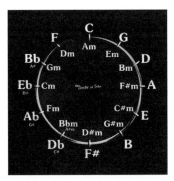

This activity offers the opportunity for collaboration between a mathematics teacher and a music teacher. It can cover several lessons, and is popular with high school students because it is a hands-on and creative application of mathematical concepts to something they all love: music. The students study how to use the Fibonacci sequence to understand mathematical concepts of patterns, recursion, Phi, and the Golden Ratio as they apply to music. You can encourage creativity by having students do choral singing, and compose an original piece of music on paper and on the keyboard. Not all students will be confident about their abilities to compose or read music, but some practice with their music-trained peers will help (adapted from Reilly, 2010).

Curriculum Objectives:

- To study new mathematical work being done today for practical applications of the Fibonacci sequence and to share the findings with the class
- To learn, understand, or review the mathematical concepts of pattern, recursion, Phi, and the Golden Ratio
- To compare and contrast two pieces of music—one of which uses the Fibonacci sequence
- To develop a set of rules for writing music using the Fibonacci sequence

Artistic Objectives:

- To use the Fibonacci sequence to play or compose music on a musical instrument, such as a xylophone or keyboard
- To identify the characteristics of music written with the Fibonacci sequence from an artistic point of view
- To sing a simple tune that uses the Fibonacci sequence

Social/Emotional Objectives:

- To collaborate with others to create a musical piece
- To practice communicating research findings and musical compositions to others

Activities: Review some history of the Fibonacci sequence and the Golden Ratio. Give the students a partially filled-in Fibonacci sequence chart and give them a set amount of time to complete it in small groups. Play the following short video to the class which shows the Fibonacci sequence in music: www.youtube.com/watch?v=2pbEarwdusc. Ask the class to pay particular attention to the repeating musical phrases as they watch the numbers on the keyboard. Ask the groups to do research on the sequence, on Phi, and on recursion. *The Fibonacci Quarterly* is an online publication that could provide good information. They should report their findings to the whole class.

Project a piano keyboard on a screen and ask questions to find out what they know about octaves, number of black-and-white keys in an octave, the pentatonic and chromatic scales. Before they write their own music, play a selection from Chopin's *Prelude No. 1 in C-Major,* which contains Fibonacci sequence and Golden Ratio patterns. Ask the class to develop a set of rules for writing music using the Fibonacci sequence. (For example, they could say this: Begin with the numbers 3, 5, 8, and 13; use the thirteen notes of the chromatic scale over eight measures; and repeat a pattern of three beats plus five beats in each measure. For the Golden Ratio, they repeat a pattern of eight notes going up and five notes going down.) They should experiment and listen to how the music sounds.

Distribute blank staff paper to the students, and ask them to compose and arrange an original musical phrase using what they have learned about the Fibonacci sequence of numbers, recursion, pattern, Phi, or the Golden Ratio. Students can work individually or in teams, but you may wish to pair students who do not know much about music with a partner who does. After writing their piece, they should experiment with it on a keyboard or xylophone, revising as needed to create an appealing sound. Students who finish early may wish to write a harmony (usually written in thirds) for their piece. Ask the students to explain the mathematical theory behind their music, and then play it for the class. They should also discuss the characteristics of their piece from an artistic perspective. You can also encourage students to sing their melodies—either alone or in a group.

You can extend this unit by suggesting that students continue to observe their surroundings for evidence of the Fibonacci sequence and to share their findings with the class. Some students may wish to write poetry using the mathematical concepts of pattern, recursion, and Golden Ratio, just as they did with music. They could also set their poem to music.

Assessment: You can use formative assessments along the way to check on student progress. If appropriate, you can ask students to evaluate their own melody. A summative assessment can follow on the mathematical concepts learned.

Materials: Music paper, simple piano sheet music, examples of musical phrases, keyboards and/or xylophones

Multiple Intelligences Addressed: Visual/Spatial, Bodily/Kinesthetic, Logical/Mathematical, Interpersonal, Intrapersonal

Bloom's Levels Addressed: Remembering, Understanding, Applying, Analyzing, Evaluating, Creating

(Note: This lesson is adapted from Reilly [2010]. ARTSEDGE and The John F. Kennedy Center for Performing Arts. Adapted with permission.)

Mathematics—Grades 9 to 10: A Geometry Field Hunt

This activity helps to show the applications of mathematics (in this case, geometry) to the real world and how it can be used in artistic projects. You can make this as simple or as complex as you wish, including having a contest to see which student identifies the greatest number of *different* geometric shapes outside the school.

Curriculum Objectives:

- To be able to identify and name different geometric shapes

- To photograph objects outside of school which contain a recognizable geometric shape

Artistic Objective:

- To recognize how geometry contributes to the creation of artistic works

Social/Emotional Objective:

- To share photos and discuss the application of geometry with other students

Activities: Review geometric terms with the class, such as a circle, cylinder, sphere, pyramid, prism, cone, arc, the three types of triangles, and various polygons. Each student uses a digital camera to take pictures of geometry in the real world. For example, a traffic pylon could be a cone, and a stop sign an octagon. Buildings often have numerous geometric shapes in their structure. The goal is to collect as many different geometric shapes in the allotted time. When finished, students load their photos into a computer and explain how each of their photos represents a specific geometric shape. One alternative to this approach would be to pick a theme either for the whole class or according to each student's interest. For example, they could look for geometry in sports, architecture, nature, or artwork.

Assessment: Use formative assessments as project progresses and a summative one to determine if students have remembered the various geometric shapes.

Materials: List of geometric terms, digital camera (preferably one for each student)

Multiple Intelligences Addressed: Visual/Spatial, Bodily/Kinesthetic, Logical/Mathematical, Interpersonal, Intrapersonal, Naturalist

Bloom's Levels Addressed: Remembering, Understanding, Applying, Analyzing, Evaluating, Creating

Mathematics—Grades 9 to 12: "Millennium Mural"

This lesson clearly shows the practical application of mathematics. Community leaders need to know how their population may change in the future in order to make appropriate plans for public services, building, zoning, and roads.

Curriculum Objectives:

- To draw and interpret graphs of relations
- To understand the notation and concept of a function, find domains and ranges, and link equations to functions
- To assess the population of their school, their town, or city
- To become familiar with the different ethnic groups, age ranges, and changes in the population in the last century, and to predict the changes in the next

Artistic Objectives:

- To learn how a mural is produced and to study famous American murals
- To apply this knowledge and contextual knowledge to analyze how content and ideas are used in works of art
- To make specific artistic choices and explain these choices throughout the creative process while defending their artistic projects

Social/Emotional Objectives:

- To recognize that communities must learn to accept diversity and to grow while accepting these differences
- To learn that their individual outlooks, interpretations, and actions can affect an entire community
- To learn that, as they create a large and permanent work of art, their collaborative final choices are just that—final choices with a permanent effect

Activities: Students research the population of their school or community over the past century or half-century, learning the ethnic make-up, age ranges, and changes in the size and makeup of the population over time. This discussion and research should lead students to predict changes in these demographics over the next century. Working in pairs, the students decide what information needs to be graphed in their notebooks. They discuss and distill their results with a historical and futuristic overview of population changes. Together, the class designs a graph, or graphs, depicting this information, using nonconventional formats (e.g., human forms instead of bars on a graph) for the graphs. They do their renderings in various ways in order to determine the final design. They discuss and choose colors and types of paint. The final step (and this takes a lot of time, so allow for it) will be the actual painting of the mural on a wall. This may be facilitated by placing the rendering onto a projector and tracing the mural onto the wall, saving a lot of time and effort. The mural can also be painted onto a canvas and hung anywhere in the school. The size of the mural must be taken into consideration. Something too tall would require the use of scaffolding or ladders, raising safety concerns. However, that may be possible, depending on the ages of your students and your particular circumstances.

Assessment: Use formative assessments throughout the project. When completed, students should be able to discuss how they use information to construct graphs and be able to interpret many types of graphs, both orally and in a traditional testing format.

Materials: Paper, notebooks, pencils, markers and crayons (for renderings), appropriate paint for a wall or canvas, drop cloths, cleanup rags, brushes, rulers, yardsticks, and a projector if necessary. (Check with your local hardware store to determine what type of paint works best on your wall or canvas.)

Multiple Intelligences Addressed: Visual/Spatial, Kinesthetic, Logical/Mathematical, Interpersonal, Intrapersonal

Bloom's Levels Addressed: Remembering, Understanding, Applying, Analyzing, Evaluating, Creating

WHAT'S COMING?

How can we create motivating STEAM lessons that use a common concept across all the K–12 grades? What are other schools doing with STEAM? What kind of professional development should we consider to successfully implement STEAM? These are some of the questions that will be answered in the next—and final—chapter.

Chapter 8—STEAM Lesson Plan Appetizers in Mathematics

Major Points to Ponder

Jot down key points, ideas, strategies, and resources that you want to consider later.

_____

_____

_____

_____

_____

_____

_____

_____

_____

_____

_____

_____

Chapter 9

Putting It
All Together

Having just a vision's no solution. Everything depends on execution:
Putting it together—that's what counts!

—Stephen Sondheim, Broadway composer

In previous chapters, we examined the impact that arts-related skills can have on activities in the STEM subjects at various grade levels. With an emphasis on creative thought through divergent thinking, teachers in the STEM areas have the opportunity to make their topics more interesting while providing students with the freedom to think, discover, and make connections across subject areas. Art is not merely for decoration or entertainment. It represents a critical part of the process of inquiry through finding and solving problems and through communication. Thus, students are more likely to understand the STEM concepts more deeply; apply them appropriately to the real world; and gain a greater appreciation of what scientists, engineers, and mathematicians actually do in their work.

In this chapter, we pull together the ideas we have already discussed and offer more suggestions for integrating arts with STEM concepts to produce STEAM lessons. But the few examples presented here show how a STEAM concept can be taught across all the elementary and secondary grade levels. Many of these concepts can also be adjusted for various levels of student interest and ability. Both gifted students and those with special needs get a new perspective on STEM topics through arts integration. As teachers get more comfortable with this approach and recognize its potential, they will expand and develop their own integrated lessons. To encourage that result, we have left some incomplete lesson plans that you can fill in with your own ideas.

We also discuss some possible formats for professional development designed to assist STEM and other curriculum area teachers in planning STEAM lessons. With all the demands placed on teachers today, we understand that they are less willing to try new ventures until they are assured of adequate support from the school administration as well as ample opportunities for professional training in the new area. Administrators should recognize that encouraging collaboration between STEM teachers and those in the arts can not only enrich the students' learning experiences but also promote a positive school culture and environment.

A FEW GENERAL GUIDELINES FOR K–12 LESSONS

Ask students to draw their observations and also write them. Drawing the idea or using color-coded keys can be powerful devices for helping students remember their learning by connecting images to words. Moreover, observational skills are as important for a successful laboratory experience as they are for a work of art.

In the upper grades, students should discuss the effectiveness of every art-based project in the form of a constructive critique. With this type of discussion, students recognize that whether the work is a laboratory report or a piece of art, it can be critically examined to ensure that observations are supported by valid reasoning. Did the project clearly convey the true structure or meaning? What was particularly effective about the project? Was there something

> *[With STEAM lessons,] students recognize that whether the work is a laboratory report or a piece of art, it can be critically examined to ensure that observations are supported by valid reasoning.*

important missing or misrepresented? Positively critiquing the project helps students to think critically, formulate questions, organize their thoughts, examine cause and effect, and synthesize what they have learned in order to construct a conclusion. It also helps them develop expressive language skills and gain a deeper scientific understanding of what they studied.

When designing these lessons, it is helpful to keep in mind the value of the Theory of Multiple Intelligences and Bloom's Taxonomy of the Cognitive Domain. These two models encourage using a variety of modalities during learning and foster the higher-order thinking that is likely to lead to creative expression. Both models have been around for a while and you may already be familiar with their design and power. Let's briefly review each one.

Theory of Multiple Intelligences

The Theory of Multiple Intelligences is a useful model for describing the various ways we process information and how we use it to direct our behavior. In 1983, Harvard psychologist Howard Gardner defined intelligence as an individual's ability to use a learned skill, create products, or solve problems in a way that is valued by the society of that individual. This approach expands our understanding of intelligence to include divergent thinking and interpersonal expertise. Gardner suggests that in everyday life people can display intelligent originality in any of seven (now eight) intelligences. They are as follows:

- *Musical/Rhythmic*—Able to create and feel a rhythm to express a mood, and to detect and analyze musical themes
- *Logical/Mathematical*—Adept at reasoning, logical thinking, and in solving mathematical problems
- *Visual/Spatial*—Create and interpret visual images, ease in thinking in three dimensions
- *Bodily/Kinesthetic*—Feels and expresses things physically and enjoys doing hands-on tasks
- *Verbal/Linguistic*—Adept at using language to express ideas, feelings, and to persuade others
- *Interpersonal (Between People)*—Understands the needs, feelings, and intentions of others
- *Intrapersonal (Within the Self)*—Clearly understand one's own thoughts and feelings
- *Naturalist*—Understands nature, and sees patterns in the way nature works (Gardner, 1993)

> *When teachers purposefully incorporate arts-related skills in their instruction, the students' benefits are abundant.*

Note how closely these intelligences correlate with the arts. For example, music requires musical/rhythmic and logical/mathematical skills. Visual art, of course, clearly calls for visual/spatial intelligence. Drama involves verbal/linguistic, bodily/kinesthetic, and interpersonal skills. Dance certainly depends on bodily/kinesthetic, visual/spatial, and interpersonal intelligences. When teachers *purposefully* incorporate arts-related skills in their instruction, the students' benefits are abundant. Gardner differentiates between the terms *intelligence* and *creativity.*

Gardner makes clear that intelligence is not just how a person thinks, but it also includes the materials and the values of the situation where and when the thinking occurs. The availability of appropriate materials and the values of any particular context or culture will thus have a significant impact on the degree to which specific intelligences will be activated, developed, or even discouraged. A person's combined intellectual capability, then, is the result of innate tendencies (the genetic contribution) and the society in which that individual develops (the environmental contribution).

This theory suggests that at the core of each intelligence is an information-processing system unique to that intelligence. The intelligence of an athlete is different from that of a musician or physicist. All can be exceptional at what they do, but different combinations of neural networks will be required to perform their tasks. Gardner also suggests that each intelligence is semi-autonomous. A person who has abilities in athletics but who does poorly in music has enhanced athletic intelligence. The presence or absence of music capabilities exists separately from the individual's athletic prowess. We find Gardner's model a useful concept for helping new and experienced teachers to understand the many ways that students can be smart. We have referred to these intelligences in a number of the activities we presented in earlier chapters.

Bloom's (Revised) Taxonomy Is Alive and Well

Gardner's model focuses on *what* information or skill the brain is processing. Other models focus on *how* the brain is working with that information or skill, such as the taxonomy of the cognitive domain proposed by psychologist Benjamin Bloom in the 1950s. His taxonomy continues to be a standard topic in many courses for prospective and practicing teachers. It has endured for more than a half century (with only one revision) because it continues to be an effective model for understanding the complexity of human thought. It is certainly not the *only* model, but it is user-friendly and simple when compared to other models. The original taxonomy contained six levels that many of you can probably recite from memory. From the least to the most complex, they were knowledge, comprehension, application, analysis, synthesis, and evaluation (Bloom, Engelhart, Furst, Hill, & Krathwohl, 1956). In 2001, a group of educators published a revision based on more recent understandings about learning (Anderson et al., 2001). The revision is shown in Figure 9.1. The dotted outline of each level suggests a more fluid model in which an individual may move among the levels during extensive cognitive processing.

In another change, synthesis exchanged places with evaluation and was renamed *create.* This exchange was made because the researchers felt that recent studies in cognitive neuroscience indicated that generating, planning, and producing an original product requires more complex thinking than making judgments based on acceptable criteria—the definition of the evaluate level.

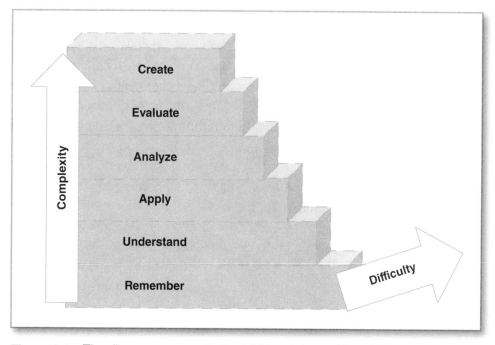

Figure 9.1   The diagram represents the 2001 revision to Bloom's Taxonomy. Notice how creating a product is now considered the highest degree of complex thinking.

Source: Adapted from Andersen et al. (2001).

The Critical Difference Between Complexity and Difficulty

Figure 9.1 shows arrows labeled "complexity" (vertical dimension) and "difficulty" (horizontal dimension). Complexity and difficulty describe different mental operations, but teachers often mistakenly consider them as synonymous. This error, resulting in the two factors being treated as one, limits the use of the taxonomy to enhance the thinking and creativity of all students, including those in the STEM areas. By recognizing how these concepts are different, the teacher can gain valuable insight into the connection between the taxonomy and student ability. Complexity describes the *thought process* that the brain uses to deal with information. In the revision of Bloom's Taxonomy, it can be described by any of the six words representing the six levels. For example, the question "What is the atomic number of oxygen?" is at the remember level, while the question "Tell me in your own words what is meant by the atomic number" is at the understand level. Thus, the second question is more complex than the first because it is at a higher level in the taxonomy: understand instead of remember.

Difficulty, on the other hand, refers to the *amount of effort* that the learner must expend *within* a level of complexity to accomplish a learning objective. It is possible for a learning activity to become increasingly difficult without becoming more complex. For example, the task "Name seven elements from the periodic table that are considered metals" is at the remember level of complexity because it involves simple recall for most students. Similarly, the task "Name seven metals and their chemical symbols" is also at the remember level but is more difficult than the prior question because it involves more effort to recall the additional information. Asking the students to "Name the first 10 elements of the periodic table and their symbols in order of their atomic numbers" is still at the remember level but is considerably more difficult than the first two. It requires gathering more information and then sequencing it in numerical order.

These are examples of how students can exert great effort to achieve a learning task while processing at the lowest level of thinking. When seeking to challenge students, classroom teachers are more likely (perhaps unwittingly) to increase difficulty rather than complexity as the challenge mode. This may be because they do not recognize the difference between these concepts or that they mistakenly believe that difficulty is the method for achieving higher-order thinking. We have referred to the levels of this model in many of the suggested activities in the previous chapters.

Sample K–12 Lessons: Examples of Arts-Related Activities in Science Topics

Simple Machines

These activities are designed to incorporate specific artists' works that have a clear connection to science.

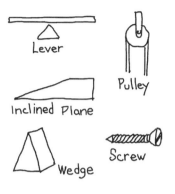

Grades K–4	Grades 5–8	Grades 9–12
Students look at pictures of simple machines and draw them, explaining what they think each part does.	Students look at, analyze, and discuss Leonardo da Vinci's inventions, asking if they work, how they work, and why. They may choose one of his machines and copy it. Using their skills of observation, students identify the parts that make the machine work and apply the appropriate scientific principles to explain how.	After viewing images of Rube Goldberg machines, students design and build their own (simplified) Rube Goldberg-like machines. They have an accompanying display, report, or presentation explaining the scientific applications of how the machine works.

Source: Portions adapted from Alberts (2008) with permission.

Observing Plants and Animals Through Journaling

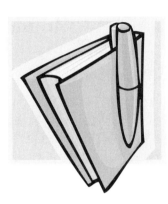

Scientists need to be able to communicate their findings to others. Keeping a journal is an important part of scientific inquiry.

Grades K–4	Grades 5–8	Grades 9–12
(See the "Inch Garden" example in Chapter 4.) Students can draw or write a play and act out a tree's life cycle.	Students examine and redraw some of the drawings of finches in Charles Darwin's book *The Origin of Species* (1859/1998) and explain how he used that evidence to develop his idea of "survival of the fittest." They then explain how important his drawings and detailed journals were to advancing scientific thought.	Students examine and discuss Meriwether Lewis's journal drawings that offer a chance to study observation and its place in American history. The importance of observation, in a time when photography had not yet been invented, can be seen in Lewis's journals. His careful observations of plant and animal species, along with descriptive writing, can be the basis of a student's own science journal.

Source: Portions adapted from Alberts (2008) with permission.

Part I of Color, Light, and Movement

Abstract examples of how science and art can interact can provide students with a deeper understanding of specific concepts.

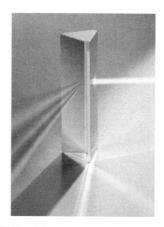

Grades K–4	Grades 5–8	Grades 9–12
The idea of color patterns in nature can be demonstrated by analyzing and discussing a Jackson Pollock painting. Students could create their own pattern drawings to emulate something in nature.	Use of color and light could be demonstrated by the pointillist paintings of Georges Seurat (1859–1891). After mixing colors on a palette, he applied dots of color to the canvas, relying on the viewer to mix the colors optically. Students could look for other examples of this technique in art or the real world.	Alexander Calder's mobiles lend themselves to the investigation of the physics of balance and movement and also to the principles behind the manipulation of the materials used: malleability and ductility. Also, an integral part of Calder's work is the shadows produced by the interaction of light with the mobile's parts.

Part II of Color, Light, and Movement

Grades K–4	Grades 5–8	Grades 9–12
Continue activities in Part I using a different artist's work.	In a unit on light, students learn the similarities between the eye and a traditional camera. The students build pinhole cameras to gain an understanding of how light rays behave. Use of prisms displays the seven colors of the visible spectrum. Students can write poems or songs to help remember ROY G BIV.	After students discuss the scientific applications behind Calder's mobiles, they use a variety of materials to make their own mobiles, and provide an explanation of the scientific applications.

Source: Portions adapted from Alberts (2008) with permission.

Periodic Table of the Elements

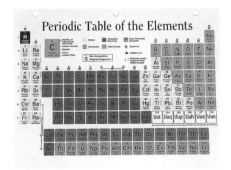

Collages allow students to gather and assemble images that represent an idea. This format appeals to students who are self-conscious about their perceived lack of artistic abilities. When students are making collages in science, the collage grows out of their completed research. This information allows students to make critical choices when looking for appropriate images to represent written facts and their research findings.

Grades K–4	Grades 5–8	Grades 9–12
Students choose an element from a list provided by the teacher who gives the students worksheets with questions about that element along with specific Internet sites to retrieve the information. Students gather their images based on their research and create a collage of images, including the name of the element.	Teacher assigns a different element to each student and gives them worksheets with questions about that element and specific Internet sites to retrieve the information. Based on their research, students create a collage of images, including the name of the element, the symbol, atomic mass, and atomic number. Teacher makes a large periodic table on the wall using the collected images. Each student presents an element and creates a brief poem, essay, or song to describe the element and explains how the selected image represents that element.	This is the same as for Grades 5–8, plus the students must explain why their element occupies its particular place in the periodic table. Students give examples of any uses that element has in the real world and, if practicable, bring in an item made of, or containing, that element.

Source: Portions adapted from Alberts (2008) with permission.

Objects in the Universe—Stained Glass Mural

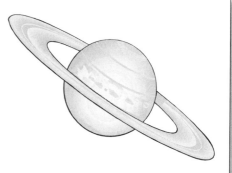

Various aspects of astronomy are covered in science lessons in elementary, middle, and high schools. This project could serve as an arts-related activity in science lessons or as a science topic in an art class. Murals are a large task to undertake. However, teachers who have done this task report that the benefits of requiring students to do deductive and inductive reasoning while collaborating on such a large project are well worth the effort and time invested.

Grades K–4	Grades 5–8	Grades 9–12
Students can work in groups and do research on a specific object in the universe. Using a printed image of their object, the group creates a collaborative drawing of their object, closely observing the differences in their images. Group members draw their images on a large piece of heavy black paper or mat board. The images are cut out, leaving a thick outline intact. Students paint tracing paper to the correct colors in the image. Tracing paper is attached to the black paper or mat board, resulting in a mural that can be placed in a window with light shining through.	This is the same as Grades K–4, plus the students write a short paper about their object. Each group presents its image to the class, and a group representative explains why they chose that object and describes some of its characteristics.	Similar to Grades 5–8, except the teacher should ensure that enough different objects are chosen, such as a planet, moon, star, nebula, etc. No two groups can have the same object. Also, student explanations should include more specific physical data (e.g., what keeps a star burning) and what scientists may know about the origin of the object. Some teachers have helped students make a film about the construction of the mural, and show it to other classes, thus enhancing their technological and communicative skills.

Source: Portions adapted from Alberts (2008) with permission.

Building Models of Cells (Plant and/or Animal)

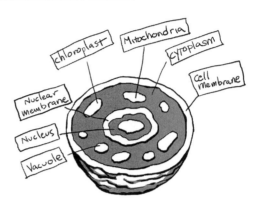

Three-dimensional models give students powerful visual and tactile representations thus allowing them to gain a better understanding of the concepts being taught. As soon as the students understand the different parts of a cell, there are several ways they can build a model. All models should be labeled and accompanied by a color-coded key.

Grades K–4	Grades 5–8	Grades 9–12
Gelatin model: Make firm gelatin (use less water) in small bowls. Students use different types of candy or fruit to represent the cell's parts and make a color-coded key describing what each piece represents.	Students work in groups and use different colors of clay to create a 3-D model of a plant *or* animal cell. Students make a color-coded key describing the cell's parts.	Students work in groups and use different colors of clay to create 3-D models of a plant *and* animal cell. Students make a color-coded key describing the cell's parts. One member from each group describes at least one difference between animal and plant cells and its implications.

Source: Portions adapted from Alberts (2008) with permission.

SAMPLE TEMPLATE FOR DESIGNING A STEAM UNIT ACROSS GRADE LEVELS

Topic:		
Grades K–4	**Grades 5–8**	**Grades 9–12**
(Activities to be conducted)	(Activities to be conducted)	(Activities to be conducted)

PROFESSIONAL DEVELOPMENT
TO MAINTAIN STEAM

This book suggests strategies that teachers can try in order to integrate arts-related skills into STEM classes: in other words, how to modify STEM into STEAM. The strategies have been derived from the current research on how we learn, especially on the recognition that creativity can be taught. Teachers who try the STEAM strategies for the first time may need support and feedback on the effectiveness of their implementation. The school-based support system is very important to maintaining teacher interest and commitment, especially if the new strategies don't produce the desired results in the classroom right away.

Role of the Building Principal/Head Teacher

Building principals and head teachers play a vital role in establishing a school climate and culture that are receptive to new instructional strategies and in maintaining the support systems necessary for continuing teacher development. Schools that develop into professional learning communities report better teacher morale, improved student achievement, and a more positive school and classroom climate (Hughes & Kritsonis, 2007). Providing opportunities for STEM teachers to master an expanded repertoire of research-based instructional techniques that include arts-related activities is an effective way for principals to foster collaboration, establish their role as an instructional leader, and enhance the teaching staff's pursuit of professional inquiry. Such opportunities can include peer coaching, in-building study groups, action research projects, and workshops that keep the faculty abreast of continuing discoveries about the teaching-learning process. For more detailed suggestions about the building principal's role, see Sousa (2003).

> *Schools that develop into professional learning communities report better teacher morale, improved student achievement, and a more positive school and classroom climate.*

Peer Coaching

Schools organized as professional learning communities find that peer coaching is an effective means of maintaining interest and furthering growth in a new instructional initiative. This structure pairs two teachers who periodically observe each other in class. During the lesson, the observing teacher is looking for the use of a particular STEAM strategy or technique that was identified in a pre-observation conference. After the lesson, the observing teacher provides feedback on the results of the implementation of the STEAM strategy. The nonthreatening and supportive nature of this peer relationship encourages teachers to take risks and to try new techniques that they might otherwise avoid for fear of failure or administrative scrutiny. Peer coaches undergo initial training in how to set the observation goal at the preconference and on different methods for collecting information during the observation.

Peer visits can become a learning experience for the observing teacher by reflecting on some questions regarding the class visited. This can be done in writing or at the post-observation conference with the teacher or teaching artist. Here are some example questions:

- What were some instructional techniques that you found interesting?
- What evidence did you have that the students were engaged in the lesson?
- What is one (or more) strategy you would like to incorporate into your own teaching?
- Is there anything else you learned from observing this class?

Study Groups

Some schools that are already using STEAM form small groups of teachers and administrators to study STEAM applications further as an effective means of expanding understanding and methods of developing new strategies. The group members seek out new research on the topic and exchange and discuss information, data, and experiences in the group setting. Each group focuses on one or two topics, such as integrating arts-related activities in science or in mathematics classes. Groups within a school or district can use cooperative learning techniques as a means of sharing information across groups.

Action Research

Fortunately, more school administrators are encouraging their teachers to engage in action research. Conducting small research studies in a class or a school can provide teachers with the validation they may need to incorporate new STEAM strategies permanently into their repertoire. Action research gives the practitioner a chance to be a researcher and to investigate specific problems that affect teaching and learning.

For example, noting whether students remember more using music to show the practical application of mathematical concepts yields data on how effective the music was in achieving a learning objective in mathematics. If several mathematics teachers carry out this research and exchange data, they will have the evidence to support the continued use of music as an effective STEAM strategy. STEM teachers can then share their results with colleagues at faculty meetings or study group sessions. This format also advances the notion that teachers should be involved in research projects as part of their professional growth.

Workshops on New Research

Periodic workshops that focus on new research findings in the teaching and learning process are valuable for updating teachers' knowledge base. One of the main reasons for encouraging arts integration is to enhance student creativity. This is an area of considerable research at this time and should be monitored to determine if new findings are appropriate for district and school workshops. True professionals are committed to updating their knowledge base constantly, and they recognize individual professional development as a personal and lifelong responsibility that will enhance their effectiveness.

Maximizing Professional Development

With tight teacher schedules and even tighter school budgets, professional development activities should be selected carefully so that they achieve a focused purpose. The primary purpose of professional development is to expand the knowledge and skills of educators so they can make decisions that are more likely to result in greater student success. This is important because all the research over the years continually points to the teacher as having the most significant school-based impact on student learning. We suggest in this book that students in STEM subjects are more likely to be successful if they are exposed to art-related skills that enhance creativity. Thus, if you are the administrator or professional development leader managing a training program to help STEM become STEAM, you might consider these tips recommended by Douglas Reeves (2010).

Focus

Consult with your STEM and arts-related teachers to determine which ones are interested in STEAM. Clearly express your expectations for the short term, and discuss what type of professional development format would work best with them.

Keep It Simple

When STEAM is the focus of the professional development, stick to it. Often, we try to cover too many topics in the same workshop and the participants feel overwhelmed. Stick with STEAM and strive for depth.

Practice

True learning is grounded in practice. Pace the training sessions so that STEM teachers have time to try out a STEAM lesson and discuss their experience at the next session. In this way, teachers have time to reflect on their implementation and look for ways to make it a permanent part of their instructional repertoire.

Prepare for Errors

Just as we should be telling students to learn from their mistakes, so should we. STEAM lessons do fail on occasion, and when they do, STEM teachers and their coaches should see this as a learning opportunity.

Do the Modeling

If you are a STEM teacher, model a STEAM lesson for the participants. Otherwise, invite some STEM teachers who are already doing STEAM lessons to do the modeling. Perhaps they can even co-teach a STEAM lesson with a willing participant. Be sure to attend the sessions with the STEM teachers and give them articles about STEAM initiatives in other schools.

Monitor Progress

Implementation of STEAM lessons is more likely to occur if teachers recognize that you will be visiting their STEAM classes and offering constructive feedback about what you observed. Using the peer coaching format, find ways for STEM teachers and teachers in the arts to observe each other periodically as they implement STEAM lessons and confer about how the lessons went.

Remove Barriers

Look ahead to what may be barriers to the implementation of STEAM lessons. Are the STEM and arts-related teachers' schedules too tight, or do they conflict and thus prohibit collaboration and peer coaching? Which of these problems are within your control, and what you can do to smooth the way? Participants need to feel that you are doing your best to make this initiative succeed. Otherwise, why should they put in their time and efforts for what they believe may be a short-lived project?

Our experience is that many STEM teachers believe they have no artistic talent and that trying to implement a STEAM lesson is bound to fail. In reality, all of us possess some degree of talent in one or more of the arts-related fields. Successful implementation of STEAM means convincing STEM teachers that they will have the support and resources needed to build upon their existing knowledge and to learn STEAM strategies.

CONCLUSION

Those of us who have been in education for more than a few decades have seen many types of instructional programs come and go. Teachers often remark about the "flavor of the year" with vestiges of the intensity and fervor of the "flavor" little more than a memory within a few years. What does remain, however, is simply "what works," and in observing thousands of teachers over the years, the thing that works best is good teacher intuition. This intuition comes from having been taught by great teachers in elementary and high school (yes, we do tend to emulate the teachers we had) and from having good, basic teaching instincts and strategies that are culled from a soupy mix of college courses. Teacher education programs in too many colleges focus heavily on educational theory rather than on encouraging growth mind-sets and on creating a blend of theory with interactive and innovative instructional strategies that have sound research to back them up. Bravo to those institutions of higher learning that have been forging ahead on this necessary and dynamic path.

At the end of the day, teaching is a great vocation. People are called to this lifelong profession with noble intent, fierce devotion, and boundless energy. Unfortunately, we continue to lose our best teachers at an alarming rate. High-stakes testing, well-meaning unions that have overreached, lack of parental and guardian support and involvement, insensitive administrations, and ill-inspired politicians are collectively causing the weakening of this wonderful vocation. As a result, we see a decline in the kind of instruction that produces creative young adults who have the capability to solve problems and who contribute to their community and to their country. Selecting a, b, or c on a test is not going to solve their real-world challenges.

From the early days of the last century through the late 1980s, students learned in schools with clear codes of conduct, caring yet strict teachers, parents and guardians who supported school policies, and plenty of

> **STEAM is a "call to arms" for an overhaul of how we train teachers and administrators, how we inform our politicians, and . . . how we significantly increase parental involvement.**

role models who had finished reconstructing an economically destroyed nation after the Great Depression and two world wars. Although our current research and understanding of how our brain learns and of what provides the best instructional strategies did not exist, somehow our schools were successful. It was called a *liberal arts education*. Building on the little scientifically based research that was available, schools created balanced instructional days including lunch and recess periods. Elementary schools typically had one teacher in the classroom, and art, art appreciation, and vocal and instrumental music classes were simply expected.

STEAM is one of the most logical concepts to come along in recent years. We need to take a liberal arts look at what and how we teach. We have mentioned in previous chapters the crying need for creativity in the classroom. STEAM is a "call to arms" for an overhaul of how we train teachers and administrators, how we inform our politicians, and—the biggest challenge of all—how we significantly increase parental involvement. In many ways, realigning the arts with the sciences puts trust back in the teachers and their capabilities and instincts and makes for a more exciting, creative, and successful classroom. And what about language arts, reading, social studies, and world languages? Perhaps in five years will we be seeing STEAM-LARSSWL. Let's hope so.

Chapter 9—Putting It All Together

Major Points to Ponder

Jot down key points, ideas, strategies, and resources that you want to consider later.

Resources

At the time of printing, reliable, noncommercial resources on STEM to STEAM were limited. Here are some that we found to be useful.

Books

Burnaford, G. E., Aprill, A., & Weiss, C. (2001). *Renaissance in the class-room: Arts integration and meaningful learning.* New York: Routledge.

This is an excellent arts integration resource with extensive details about programs done at the Chicago Arts Partnership in Education.

Donahue, D. M., & Stuart, J. (Eds.). (2010). *Artful teaching: Integrating the arts for understanding across the curriculum, K–8.* New York: Teachers College Press.

Films

Something Within Me (Available on Netflix)

This 1993 inspiring documentary by Emma Joan Morris is about a poor Catholic school in the South Bronx where many children were failing miserably at basic academics. The administrators of St. Augustine's (including one of the authors of this book) tried a new approach. They revamped the curriculum to stress the arts, particularly music. As students became involved with their instruments, their test scores went up. This uplifting film won three awards at the Sundance Film Festival.

Journals

Children's Technology and Engineering
   www.iteea.org/Publications/t&c.htm
   This quarterly journal focuses on teaching technology in elementary schools and includes articles that provide practical and creative ideas and activities for the elementary classroom teacher. It also provides updates on the progress of interdisciplinary learning programs among other similar issues.

Journal of Mathematics and the Arts
   www.tandfonline.com/toc/tmaa20/current
   This quarterly peer-reviewed journal contains articles of interest to those who use mathematics in the creation of their art. It includes artists' descriptions of the mathematical context of their work, ideas that mathematics and arts teachers can use for interdisciplinary lessons, and insights about art and mathematics different settings.

Teaching Artist Journal
   http://tajournal.com
   This is a print and online quarterly that serves as a voice, forum, and resource for teaching artists and for all those working at the intersection of art and learning.

Organizations

The Arts and Science Council
   227 W. Trade Street, Suite 250
   Charlotte, North Carolina 28202
   704-333-2ASC (2272)
   This is a public agency of the city of Charlotte, North Carolina, and Mecklenburg County that has information about grant opportunities, public art, professional services, and cultural education. Its site also includes suggestions for integrating the arts and sciences in classroom instruction.

Association of Teaching Artists
   www.teachingartists.com
   This is a great source for teaching artist resources with good hyperlinks to other arts education and arts integration sites.

Perpich Center for Arts Education

www.pcae.k12.mn.us/pdr/pdr_legacy.html

This center has established a special initiative for arts integration in K–12 schools in several Minnesota districts. The Perpich Arts Integration Network of Teachers (PAINT) works with teachers to develop and implement arts-integrated lessons into other content area courses. The website explains the various aspects of the program.

Common Core State Standards

Common Core State Standards (CCSS) in Mathematics

www.corestandards.org/assets/CCSSI_Math%20Standards.pdf

As of this writing, the CCSS in mathematics have been adopted by forty-eight states (not adopted in Alaska and Texas). The full text of the standards in mathematics can be found on the website.

Next Generation Science Standards

www.nextgenscience.org

New K–12 science standards are currently being developed. As a result of the first public comment phase, they are being rewritten and will be submitted to each state for review.

Websites

Arts Edge at the Kennedy Center

http://artsedge.kennedy-center.org/educators.aspx

This valuable resource site has numerous lessons, activities, and projects designed to integrate the arts with other curriculum areas. Lesson plans are very detailed with hyperlinks to other sites.

ARTStem

http://artstem.org

ARTStem is a project from the University of North Carolina School of the Arts that helps public school educators promote collaborations that explore the relationship between learning and teaching in the arts and the so-called STEM disciplines. Its objective is to generate a series of faculty projects that will bring the arts-integrated STEM activities to a broader set of students, instructors, and staff at both the university and the public schools involved. The website offers many videos, research articles, and explanations of ARTStem projects currently underway.

Center for Creative Education
    425 24th St.
    West Palm Beach, Florida 33407
    http://cceflorida.org
A great resource for ideas on arts integration lesson plans. Move around the site to view the instructional units available through their CADRE program for good ideas.

Chicago Arts Partnerships in Education
    http://CAPEweb.org
This is one of the leading arts integration organizations in the country. You can review lesson plans that include descriptions of how well the lesson plans worked.

STEM to STEAM
    http://stemtosteam.org
This website is sponsored by the Rhode Island School of Design (RISD), which is sponsoring the STEAM initiative in order to stimulate innovation and creativity in students.

Wolf Trap Foundation for the Performing Arts
    www.wolftrap.org
This nonprofit foundation launched an innovative Early Childhood STEM Learning Through the Arts initiative that builds upon its thirty-year history developing and delivering early childhood arts education programs. The foundation has partnered with the Fairfax County Public Schools in Virginia and the American Institute for Research to develop, evaluate, and disseminate arts-based STEM teaching strategies for pre-K and kindergarten.

References

Alberts, R. (2008). *Discovering science through art-based activities.* Retrieved June 12, 2012, from http://beyondpenguins.ehe.osu.edu/issue/earths-changing-surface/discovering-science-through-art-based-activities.

Anderson, L. W. (Ed.), Krathwohl, D. R. (Ed.), Airasian, P. W., Cruikshank, K. A., Mayer, R. E., Pintrich, P. R., et al. (2001). *A taxonomy for learning, teaching, and assessing: A revision of Bloom's Taxonomy of Educational Objectives* (Complete edition). New York: Longman.

Andiliou, A., & Murphy, P. K. (2010). Examining variations among researchers' and teachers' conceptualizations of creativity: A review and synthesis of contemporary research. *Educational Research Review, 5*(3), 201–219.

Andreasen, N. C. (2005). *The creating brain: The neuroscience of genius.* New York: Dana Press.

Armstrong, T. (1991). *Awakening your child's natural genius.* New York: Tarcher/Putnam.

Aud, S., Hussar, W., Kena, G., Bianco, K., Frohlich, L., Kemp, J., et al. (2011, May). *The condition of education: 2011.* Washington, DC: U.S. Department of Education, National Center for Education Statistics.

Barrow, L. H. (2010). Encouraging creativity with scientific inquiry. *Creative Education, 1,* 1–6.

Beghetto, R. A. (2006). Creative justice? The relationship between prospective teachers' prior schooling experiences and perceived importance of promoting student creativity. *Journal of Creative Behavior, 40*(3), 149–162.

Bloom, B. S. (Ed.), Engelhart, M. D., Furst, E. J., Hill, W. H., & Krathwohl, D. R. (1956). *Taxonomy of educational objectives: The classification of educational goals. Handbook I: Cognitive domain.* New York: David McKay.

Brown, E. D., Benedett, B., & Armistead, M. E. (2010). Arts enrichment and school readiness for children at risk. *Early Childhood Research Quarterly, 25*(1), 112–124.

Bushaw, W. J., & Lopez, S. J. (2011). *Betting on teachers: The 43rd annual Phi Delta Kappa/Gallup Poll of the public's attitudes toward the public schools.* Bloomington, IN: Phi Delta Kappa.

Campbell, S. (2006). Language in the nondominant hemisphere. In K. Brown (Ed.), *Encyclopedia of language and linguistics* (2nd ed., pp. 529–536). Oxford, UK: Elsevier.

Catterall, J. S. (with Dumais, S. A., & Hampden-Thompson, G.). (2012). *The arts and achievement in at-risk youth: Findings from four longitudinal studies.* Washington, DC: National Endowment for the Arts.

Centers for Disease Control and Prevention. (2010). *The association between school based physical activity, including physical education, and academic performance.* Atlanta, GA: U.S. Department of Health and Human Services.

Chan, A. S., Ho, Y. C., & Cheung, M. C. (1998). Music training improves verbal memory, *Nature, 396,* 128.

Change the Equation. (2012). *Stem help wanted: Demand for science, technology, engineering and mathematics weathers the storm.* Retrieved October 1, 2012, from http://changetheequation.org/sites/default/files/CTEq_VitalSigns_Supply %20%282%29. Pdf.

Chapman, C., Laird, J., Ifill, N., & KewalRamani, A. (2011). *Trends in high school dropout and completion rates in the United States: 1972–2009* (NCES 2012–006). Washington, DC: National Center for Education Statistics.

Chávez-Eakle, R. A., Graff-Guerrero, A. G., García-Reyna, J. C., Vaugier, V., & Cruz-Fuentes, C. (2007, November). Cerebral blood flow associated with creative performance: A comparative study. *NeuroImage, 38,* 519–528.

Chen, I. (2009, June). Brain cells for socializing: Does an obscure nerve cell explain what gorillas, elephants, whales—and people—have in common? *Smithsonian,* 38–43.

Complete College America. (2012, April). *Remediation: Higher education's bridge to nowhere.* Washington, DC: Author.

Darwin, C. (1998). *The origin of species.* New York: Oxford University Press. (Original work published 1859)

Devlin, K. (2000). *The math gene: How mathematical thinking evolved and why numbers are like gossip.* New York: Basic Books.

Diamond, A., Barnett, W. S., Thomas, J., & Munro, S. (2007, November). Preschool program improves cognitive control. *Science, 318,* 1387–1388.

Diamond, J. (1992). *The third chimpanzee: The evolution and future of the human animal.* New York: Harper Perennial.

Dokoupil, T. (2012, July 19). Tweets, texts, email, posts: Is the onslaught making us crazy? *Newsweek, CLX,* 24–30.

Duckworth, A. L., Peterson, C., Matthews, M. D., & Kelly, D. R. (2007). Grit: Perseverance and passion for long-term goals. *Journal of Personality and Social Psychology, 92*(6), 1087–1101.

Duffau, H., Leroy, M., & Gatignol, P. (2008, December). Cortico-subcortial organization of language networks in the right hemisphere: An electrostimulation study in left-handers. *Neuropsychologia, 46,* 3197–3209.

Dweck, C. S. (2006). *Mindset: The new psychology of success.* New York: Random House.

Eisner, E. (2002a). *The arts and the creation of mind.* New Haven, CT: Yale University Press.

Eisner, E. (2002b). What the arts do for the young. *School Arts, 102,* 16–17.

Elder, C. A., & Obel-Omia, M. C. (2012). Why bother with recess? *Education Week, 31*(30), 27.

Ellis, A. W., Ansorge, L., & Lavidor, M. (2007, December). Words, hemispheres, and dissociable subsystems: The effects of exposure duration, case alternation, and continuity of form on word recognition in the left and right visual fields. *Brain and Language, 103,* 292–303.

Ewald, E., & Gerlman, J. (2010). *Alexander Calder: Master of balance. How do balance and motion connect art and science?* Retrieved August 11, 2012, from http://artsedge.kennedy-center.org/educators/lessons/grade-5/Alexander_ Calder_ Master_of_Balance.aspx. Adapted with permission.

Fink, A., Benedek, M., Grabner, R. H., Staudt, B., & Neubauer, A, C. (2007). Creativity meets neuroscience: Experimental tasks for the neuroscientific study of creative thinking. *Methods, 42*(1), 68–76.

Florida Department of Education. (n.d.). Next Generation Sunshine State Standards. Retrieved December 5, 2012, from www.fldoe.org/bii/curriculum/sss/

Gardner, H. (1983). *Frames of mind: The theory of multiple intelligences.* New York: Basic Books.

Gardner, H. (1993). *Frames of mind: The theory of multiple intelligences* (Rev. ed.). New York: Basic Books.

Hadamard, J. (1954). *An essay on the psychology of invention in the mathematical field.* New York: Dover Publications.

Haley, J. A. (2001). The relationship between instrumental music instruction and academic achievement in fourth grade students. (Doctoral dissertation, Pace University, 2001). *Dissertation Abstracts International, 62*(09), 2969A.

Hecht, D. (2010, October). Depression and the hyperactive right-hemisphere. *Neuroscience Research, 68,* 77–87.

Heilman, K. M., Nadeau, S. E., Beversdorf, D. O. (2003). Creative innovation: Possible brain mechanisms. *Neurocase, 9,* 369–379.

Heimann, M., Tjus, T., & Strid, K. (2010). Attention in cognition and early learning. *International Encyclopedia of Education,* 165–171.

Ho, Y. C., Cheung, M. C., & Chan, A. S. (2003). Music training improves verbal but not visual memory: Cross sectional and longitudinal explorations in children. *Neuropsychology, 17,* 439–450.

Hughes, T. A., & Kritsonis, W. A. (2007). *Professional learning communities and the positive effects on achievement: A national agenda for school improvement.* Retrieved August 12, 2012, from www.allthingsplc.info/pdf/articles/plcand thepositiveeffects.pdf.

Hyde, K. L., Lerch, J., Norton, A., Forgeard, M., Winner, E., Evans, A. C., et al. (2009, March). Musical training shapes structural brain development. *The Journal of Neuroscience, 29*(10), 3019–3025.

Ingersoll, R., Merrill, L., & May, H. (2012, May). Retaining teachers: How preparation matters. *Educational Leadership, 69*(8), 30–34.

Jauk, E., Benedek, M., & Neubauer, A. C. (2012, May). Tackling creativity at its roots: Evidence for different patterns of EEG activity related to convergent and divergent modes of task processing. *International Journal of Psychophysiology, 84,* 219–225.

Johnson, C. M., & Memmott, J. E. (2006). Examination of relationships between music programs of differing quality and standardized test results. *Journal of Research in Music Education, 54*(4), 293–307.

Jung-Beeman, M., Bowden, E. M., Haberman, J., Frymiare, J. L., Arambel-Liu, S., Greenblatt, R., et al. (2004). Neural Activity When People Solve Verbal Problems with Insight. *Public Library of Science—Biology, 2*(4), e97.

Kampylis, P., Berki, E., & Sarriluoma, P. (2009, April). In-service and prospective teachers' perceptions of creativity. *Thinking Skills and Creativity, 4*(1), 15–29.

Kener, D. (2012). Drama week on the Learning Network. *The New York Times Learning Network.* Retrieved August 6–10, 2012, from http://learning.blogs.nytimes.com.

Koutsoupidou, T., & Hargreaves, D. (2009). An experimental study of the effects of improvisation on the development of children's creative thinking in music. *Psychology of Music, 37*(3), 251–278.

Kraft, U. (2007). Unleashing creativity. In F. Bloom (Ed.), *Best of the brain from Scientific American: Mind, matter, and tomorrow's brain* (pp. 9–19). New York: Dana Press.

Lehrer, J. (2012a). *Imagine: How creativity works.* New York: Houghton Mifflin Harcourt.

Lehrer, J. (2012b). Interview with Charlie Rose on April 17, 2012. Retrieved from www.charlierose.com/view/interview/12302.

Limb, C. J., & Braun, A. R. (2008). Neural substrates of spontaneous musical performance: An fMRI study of jazz improvisation. *PLoS ONE 3*(2), e1679.

Loveless, T. (2012). *The 2012 Brown Center Report on American education: How well are American students learning?* Washington, DC: The Brookings Institution.

Maguire, E. A., Gadian, D. G., Johnsrude, I. S., Good, C. D., Ashburner, J., Frackowiak, R. S. J., et al. (2000, April 11). Navigation-related structural changes in the hippocampi of taxi drivers. *Proceedings of the National Academy of Sciences USA, 97*(8), 4398–4403.

McPherson, G. E., & Hendricks, K. S. (2010, December). Students' motivation to study music: The United States of America. *Research Studies in Music Education, 32,* 201–213.

Meier, D. (1995). *The power of their ideas: Lessons for America from a small school in Harlem.* Boston, MA: Beacon Press.

MetLife survey of the American teacher. (2012). New York: Metropolitan Life Insurance Company.

Middleton, M. C. (2008). *Art interest inventory.* Wando High School, Charleston, SC: Author.

National Assessment of Educational Progress. (2012). *2011 Grade 8 science assessments.* Washington, DC: U.S. Department of Education.

National Center for Education Statistics. (2012). *Science in action: Hands-on and interactive computer tasks from the 2009 science assessment* (NCES 2012–468). Washington, DC: U.S. Department of Education.

National Research Council. (2012). *A framework for K–12 science education: Practices, crosscutting concepts, and core ideas.* Washington, DC: The National Academies Press.

Organisation for Economic Co-operation and Development. (2011). *Education at a Glance 2011: OECD Indicators.* Paris: Organization for Economic Cooperation and Development Publishing.

Park, M.-H., Park, E.-J., Choi, J., Chai, S., Lee, J.-H., Lee, C., et al. (2011, December). Preliminary study of Internet addiction and cognitive function in adolescents based on IQ tests. *Psychiatry Research, 190,* 275–281.

Parsad, B., & Lewis, L. (2006). *Calories in, calories out: Food and exercise in public elementary schools, 2005* (NCES 2006–057). Washington, DC: National Center for Education Statistics.

Parsad, B., & Spiegelman, M. (2012). *Arts education in public elementary and secondary schools: 1999–2000 and 2009–10* (NCES 2012–014). Washington, DC: National Center for Education Statistics.

Piro, J. M., & Ortiz, C. (2009). The effect of piano lessons on the vocabulary and verbal sequencing skills of primary grade students. *Psychology of Music, 37*(3), 325–347.

Popham, W. J. (2008). *Transformative assessment.* Alexandria, VA: Association for Supervision and Curriculum Development.

Posner, M., Rothbart, M. K., Sheese, B. E., & Kieras, J. (2008). How arts training influences cognition. In C. Asbury & B. Rich (Eds.), *Learning, arts, and the brain* (pp. 1–10). New York: Dana Press.

Ramey, L. K. (2005). *Examination of the impact of involvement in the arts on students' decision to stay in school.* Dayton, OH: Wright State University. (ERIC Document Reproduction Service No. ED490785)

Reeves, D. (2010). *Transforming professional development into student success.* Alexandria, VA: ASCD.

Register, D. (2001). The effects of an early intervention music curriculum on prereading/writing. *Journal of Music Therapy, 38*(3), 239–248.

Reilly, A. (2010). *Amazing Fibonacci: How the hidden life of numbers make memorable music.* Retrieved August 12, 2012, from http://artsedge.kennedy-center.org/educators/lessons/grade-9-12/Fibonacci_Music.aspx. Adapted with permission.

Rinne, L., Gregory, E., Yarmolinskaya, J., & Hardiman, M. (2011). Why arts integration improves long-term retention of content. *Mind, Brain, and Education, 5*(2), 89–96.

Root-Bernstein, R. S. (1997, July 11). Art for science's sake. *Chronicle of Higher Education,* p. B6.

Sandkühler, S., & Bhattacharya, J. (2008, January). Deconstructing insight: EEG correlates of insightful problem solving. *Public Library of Science ONE,* 10.1371/journal.pone.0001459.

Schellenberg, E. G. (2003). Does exposure to music have beneficial side effects? In I. Peretz & R. J. Zatorre (Eds.), *The cognitive neuroscience of music* (pp. 430–448). Oxford, UK: Oxford University Press.

Schellenberg, E. G. (2004). Music lessons enhance IQ. *Psychological Science, 15*(8), 511–514.

Schlaug, G., Jäncke, L., Huang, Y., Staiger, J. F., & Steinmetz, H. (1995, August). Increased corpus callosum size in musicians. *Neuropsychologia, 33,* 1047–1055.

Seeley, W. W., Matthews, B. R., Crawford, R. K., Gorno-Tempini, M. L., Foti, D., Mackenzie, I. R., et al. (2008). Unravelling Bolero: Progressive aphasia, transmodal creativity and the right posterior neocortex. *Brain, 131,* 39–49.

Snyder, A., & Raichle, M. (2012, August). A brief history of the resting state: The Washington University perspective. *NeuroImage,62,* 902–910.

Sousa, D. A. (2003). *The leadership brain: How to lead today's schools more effectively.* Thousand Oaks, CA: Corwin Press.

Sousa, D. A. (2008). *How the brain learns mathematics.* Thousand Oaks, CA: Corwin Press.

Sousa, D. A., & Tomlinson, C. A. (2011). *Differentiation and the brain: How neuroscience supports the learner-friendly classroom.* Bloomington, IN: Solution Tree Press.

Standley, J. M., & Hughes, J. E. (1997). Evaluation of an early intervention music curriculum for enhancing prereading/writing skills. *Music Therapy Perspectives, 15*(2), 79–85.

Stromberg, J. (2012, July 25). *When the Olympics gave out medals for art.* Retrieved July 29, 2012, from www.smithsonianmag.com/arts-culture/When-the-Olympics-Gave-Out-Medals-for-Art-163705106.html.

Sylwester, R. (2007). *The adolescent brain: Reaching for autonomy.* Thousand Oaks, CA: Corwin.

Sylwester, R. (2010). *A child's brain: The need for nurture.* Thousand Oaks, CA: Corwin.

Takeuchi, H., Taki, Y., Sassa, Y., Hashizume, H., Sekiguchi, A., Fukushima, A., et al. (2010, May). White matter structures associated with creativity: Evidence from diffusion tensor imaging. *NeuroImage, 51*(1), 11–18.

Toyoshima, K., Fukui, H., & Kuda, K. (2011, August). Piano playing reduces stress more than other creative art activities. *International Journal of Music Education, 29,* 257–263.

Turkle, S. (2011). *Alone together: Why we expect more from technology and less from each other.* New York: Basic Books.

U.S. Department of Education. (2011). U.S. Department of Education, *The condition of education 2011* (NCES 2011–033), Indicator 21. Washington, DC: National Center for Education Statistics.

Valcke, M., De Wever, B., Van Keer, H., & Schellens, T. (2011, August). Long-term study of safe Internet use of young children. *Computers & Education, 57,* 1292–1305.

Wagner, U., Gais, S., Haider, H., Verleger, R., & Born, J. (2004, January). Sleep inspires insight. *Nature, 427,* 352–355.

Whitehead, B. J. (2001). The effect of music-intensive intervention on mathematics scores of middle and high school students (Doctoral dissertation, Capella University, 2001). *Dissertation Abstracts International, 62*(08), 2710A.

Yager, R. E. (2007, October). STS requires changes in teaching. *Bulletin of Science, Technology, & Society, 27,* 386–390.

Zamarian, L., Ischebeck, A., & Delazer, M. (2009, June). Neuroscience of learning arithmetic: Evidence from brain imaging studies. *Neuroscience & Biobehavioral Reviews, 33,* 909–925.

Zhou, Y., Lin, F.-C., Du, Y.-S., Qin, L.-D., Zhao, Z.-M., Xu, J.-R., et al. (2011, July). Gray matter abnormalities in Internet addiction: A voxel-based morphometry study. *European Journal of Radiology, 79,* 92–95.

Index

CORWIN

A SAGE Company

The Corwin logo—a raven striding across an open book—represents the union of courage and learning. Corwin is committed to improving education for all learners by publishing books and other professional development resources for those serving the field of PreK–12 education. By providing practical, hands-on materials, Corwin continues to carry out the promise of its motto: **"Helping Educators Do Their Work Better."**